LEBANON
in Pictures

Margaret J. Goldstein

Lerner Publications Company

Contents

Lerner Publishing Group realizes that current information and statistics quickly become out of date. To extend the usefulness of the Visual Geography Series, we developed www.vgsbooks.com, a website offering links to up-to-date information, as well as in-depth material, on a wide variety of subjects. All of the websites listed on www.vgsbooks.com have been carefully selected by researchers at Lerner Publishing Group. However, Lerner Publishing Group is not responsible for the accuracy or suitability of the material on any website other than <www.lernerbooks.com>. It is recommended that students using the Internet be supervised by a parent or teacher. Links on www.vgsbooks.com will be regularly reviewed and updated as needed.

Website address: www.lernerbooks.com

Lerner Publications Company
A division of Lerner Publishing Group
241 First Avenue North
Minneapolis, MN 55401 U.S.A.

J 915.692
Goldstein

CULTURAL LIFE ▸ 46

► Language and Literature. Performing Arts. Art and Architecture. Modern Media. Foods of Lebanon. Holidays and Festivals. Sports and Recreation.

THE ECONOMY ▸ 58

► Services. Industry and Agriculture. Transportation. Future Challenges.

FOR MORE INFORMATION

Library of Congress Cataloging-in-Publication Data

Goldstein, Margaret J.
    Lebanon in pictures / by Margaret J. Goldstein.
        p.   cm. – (Visual geography series)
    Includes bibliographical references and index.
    ISBN: 0-8225-1171-1 (lib. bdg. : alk. paper)
    1. Lebanon—Juvenile literature. [1. Lebanon.] I. Title. II. Series: Visual geography series (Minneapolis, Minn.)
    DS80.G65 2005
    956.92—dc22   2003026471

Manufactured in the United States of America
1 2 3 4 5 6 - JR - 10 09 08 07 06 05

INTRODUCTION

The Republic of Lebanon is a small Middle Eastern nation on the eastern edge of the Mediterranean Sea. It became an independent republic in 1943, but its history is thousands of years older. Historians have found evidence that people lived in the region in prehistoric times. Lebanon's earliest known inhabitants, the Canaanites, settled the land in about 3000 B.C. The Canaanites were followed by the Phoenicians, who moved into the region in about 2500 B.C.

From their cities along the Mediterranean seacoast, the Phoenicians became a great trading people. Phoenician sailors, merchants, and explorers traveled and did business in Europe, Asia, and North Africa, as well as in other parts of the Middle East. The Phoenicians developed a writing system that became the basis for our modern Roman alphabet.

But the Phoenicians did not have a centralized government or a strong leader. They were vulnerable to foreign conquerors. As a result, the area that would become Lebanon was conquered first by the

Egyptians, and later by the Greeks, the Romans, the Arabs, the Christians, the Ottomans, and several other foreign powers. In its more than five thousand years of history, Lebanon has mostly been ruled by other, stronger nations.

Lebanon finally won its independence in the mid-twentieth century, but the new nation faced many struggles afterward. Its population was split between Muslims (people who follow the Islamic religion) and Christians. In addition to their religious differences, these groups held contrasting cultural and political views. The Christians had ties to the United States and other Western nations. The Muslims felt kinship with the rest of the Middle East, where Islam is the dominant religion. This division soon led to armed conflict, the first time in 1958.

In the late 1960s, the political situation became more complicated. Since 1948 thousands of Palestinians had been living in Lebanon. The Palestinians were primarily Muslims who had fled their homes in

SYRIA

NORTH LEBANON

Musa River

Abu Ali River

• Tripoli

MEDITERRANEAN SEA

Palm Islands Reserve

• Shikka

Amyun

Horsh Ehden Nature Reserve

• Bsharri

Orontes River

Byblos

Jubayl

Ibrahim River

BEKAA

∴• Baalbek

Juniyah

MOUNT LEBANON

Beirut

• Borj Hammoud

Burj al Barajinah •

BEIRUT

Zahlé

Aanjar

Litani River

Chouf Cedar Reserve

Beiteddine

Awwali River

Lake Qaraoun

Sidon

Jazzïn

SYRIA

NABATIYAH

∴ Tyre

SOUTH LEBANON

ISRAEL

JORDAN

Lebanon

— International border

— · — Province border

✪ Capital city

• City

∴ Archaeological site

0   20 Miles

0   20 KM

N

Palestine during the war for Israeli independence that year. Hoping to regain their former territory, Palestinian fighters based in Lebanon attacked Israel to the south. Many Lebanese Christians opposed the Palestinian fighters, while many Lebanese Muslims supported them. The conflict soon erupted into a full-scale civil war that lasted throughout the 1980s. A 1991 peace plan put an end to the major fighting, but deep religious and political rivalries continued to plague the nation. In addition, Lebanon emerged from the civil war with a badly damaged economy. Over the course of the decade, Lebanon's leaders and citizens worked to rebuild their nation. The economy improved. Businesses and tourists, who had left during the war, returned.

Visitors to twenty-first century Lebanon will find it has a fascinating history dating back thousands of years. It has a thriving modern culture that skillfully blends old and new, East and West. In the capital city of Beirut, visitors can see centuries-old buildings standing in the shadows of gleaming, modern skyscrapers. Ruins of some of the world's oldest cities are found along the coast. Lebanese artisans draw on ancient techniques to produce exquisite glassware, silverware, and jewelry. Lebanese cooks use recipes passed down through the generations to prepare tasty and spicy meals.

Lebanon sits in the heart of the Middle East, a region plagued by wars, terrorism, and political struggle. Despite the conflicts that surround them, the Lebanese people carry on their work and family life with dreams of a more peaceful tomorrow. Although their nation has been damaged by war, their skills, spirit, and traditions are strong. The Lebanese people are hopeful that these strengths will carry them into a brighter future.

THE LAND

Lebanon lies at the eastern end of the Mediterranean Sea. It has about 4,000 square miles (10,360 square kilometers) of territory—an area slightly smaller than the state of Connecticut. On a map, it is roughly rectangular in shape, 135 miles (217 km) long and only 20 to 55 miles (32 to 88 km) wide. It is bounded on the north and east by Syria, on the south by Israel, and on the west by the Mediterranean Sea.

Geographical Regions

Lebanon consists of four geographical regions. From west to east these regions are the Coastal Plain, the Lebanon Mountains, the Bekaa Valley, and the Anti-Lebanon Mountains.

The Coastal Plain is a narrow strip of land running north to south along the Mediterranean Sea. At its widest, the plain is only 8 miles (13 km) across. In places where the mountains drop steeply to the sea, the plain disappears altogether. The plain has fertile land for farming and sheltered bays where ships can drop anchor. Since ancient times,

these features have made the plain attractive to settlers. Most of Lebanon's major cities are located on this plain.

Mountains run nearly the entire length of Lebanon, from the Syrian border in the north to the Israeli border in the south. To the east of the seacoast, the Lebanon Mountains rise sharply, towering steeply above the Coastal Plain. The highest mountain in the country—Qurnat as Sawda—stands in the northern part of the range. It peaks at 10,115 feet (3,083 meters) above sea level. The Lebanon Mountains receive plentiful snowfall in winter. Several ski resorts are located among the tallest peaks. The Chouf Mountains, found in the southern part of the range, are home to most of Lebanon's famous cedar trees. The mountains decrease in height the farther you travel south.

The Bekaa Valley runs along the east side of the Lebanon Mountains. The valley is 75 miles (120 km) long and 5 to 10 miles (8 to 16 km) wide. It is part of the Great Rift Valley, a series of valleys that run from Syria down into southeastern Africa. Many rivers run into the valley from the surrounding mountains. These rivers make the valley moist and fertile. It is a good crop-growing region, and agriculture thrives there.

The Anti-Lebanon Mountains make up the easternmost region of the country. They extend along Lebanon's eastern border with Syria and south into Israel. The highest peak in the Lebanese section of the range is Mount Hermon, standing 9,232 feet (2,814 m) above sea level. It sits in the southern part of the country, straddling the Lebanon-Syria border.

Rivers

Two major rivers run the length of Lebanon, providing plentiful water for farming. The Litani River begins in the Bekaa Valley near the ancient town of Baalbek and flows southward, cutting through the Lebanon Mountains and then emptying into the sea just north of Tyre. In the middle of its course, near the Chouf Cedar Reserve, the Litani widens considerably, forming a small lake called Lake Qaraoun.

The Orontes River flows northward from the Lebanon Mountains into Syria. Other rivers, including the Musa, Ibrahim, and Awwali, flow from the Lebanon Mountains westward into the sea. Many rivers in Lebanon are seasonal. They flow in the spring, when snow melts in the surrounding mountains. Much of the rest of the year, the rivers are dry streambeds.

The **Litani River** provides water for many crops.

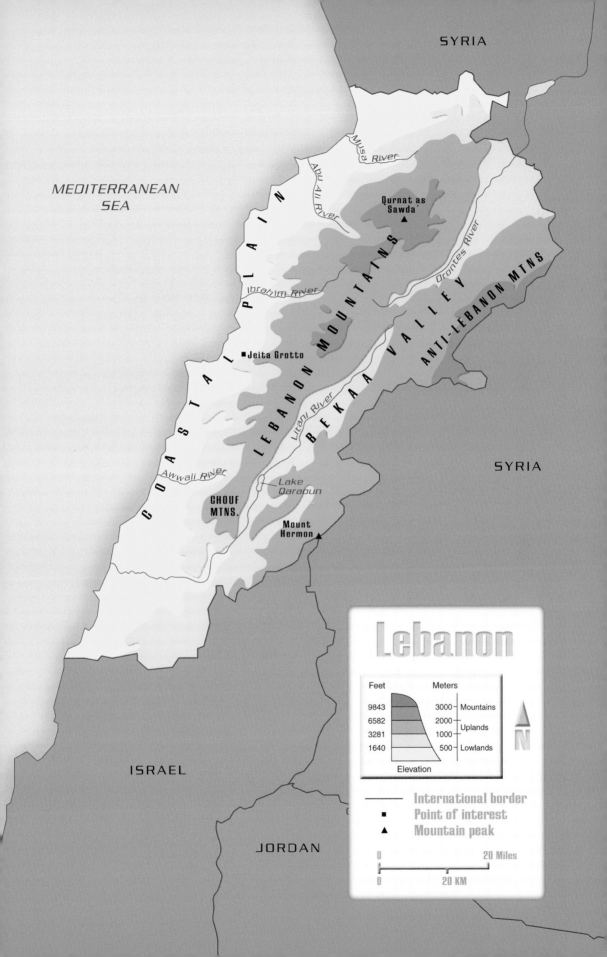

◎ Climate

The weather varies in Lebanon, depending on geographical region. The coast has a mild climate, with cool, rainy winters and warm summers. Winter temperatures on the coast average about 56°F (14°C), while summer temperatures average around 86°F (30°C). Summers on the coast tend to be muggy, or humid, with warm, moist breezes blowing in from the Mediterranean Sea.

The weather is much cooler in Lebanon's two mountain ranges. Winter averages are just 36°F (2°C), with 70°F (21°C) averages in summer. The Bekaa Valley climate falls somewhere in between the mountains and the coast, with summertime temperatures averaging about 80°F (27°C) and winter averages around 48°F (9°C).

Most of Lebanon's rain falls in January and February, during the winter rainy season. Summers are very dry. The mountains receive 50 to 60 inches (127 to 152 centimeters) of rain each year, with heavy snowfalls in winter. The coast receives about 35 inches (89 cm) of rain a year. The Bekaa Valley tends to be drier than the coast and the mountains, because the Lebanon Mountains block moist winds blowing in off the sea. Little rain falls on the valley in summer. Winters there sometimes have frost and snow.

> At its widest only 55 miles (88 km) across, Lebanon is a very small country. Tourist brochures boast that you can swim in the sea and ski in the mountains all in the same day in Lebanon, and indeed you can—part of the year. The nation has six ski resorts, and the ski season lasts from November to May.

◎ Flora and Fauna

Lebanon's most famous plants (flora) are its cedar trees. These trees once grew in great abundance on the upper slopes of the Lebanon Mountains. But since ancient times, the trees have been steadily cut down. In past eras, many foreign rulers built their palaces from the trees' sturdy, fragrant wood. As a result, few cedar groves remain in Lebanon, although the cedar tree remains Lebanon's national symbol.

Over the years, cedar and other varieties of trees have been cut for construction material and firewood and to clear land for farming. Some trees were destroyed by gunfire and explosives during the long years of civil war. Still, some woodlands remain, and Lebanon is the most heavily wooded of all Middle Eastern countries. In addition to the surviving cedar groves (mostly found in the Chouf Mountains), Lebanon has stands of pine, juniper, oak, fir, beech, and cypress trees

in the mountains. Orange, lemon, banana, palm, and olive trees grow along the coast. Few trees grow in the Bekaa Valley, which instead features irrigated vegetable fields and vineyards (fields of grapevines).

A variety of smaller plants, including poppies, anemones (a kind of buttercup), wild herbs, and thorny shrubs, grow throughout the nation. In spring the nation's mountains and hills come to life with wildflowers, including the colorful Lebanon violet.

The animal life (fauna) of Lebanon is also diverse. Deer live in the mountains, along with wild cats, porcupines, badgers, foxes, squirrels, hedgehogs, and hares. Wolves, wild boars, wild goats, and gazelles live in the Chouf Cedar Reserve in the Chouf Mountains. But due to hunting and the destruction of their natural homes, some of these animals are increasingly rare in Lebanon.

Flamingos, pelicans, ducks, and herons inhabit the marshes of the Bekaa Valley. All of these birds are migratory, flying south in autumn and north in spring. Storks,

THE CEDARS OF LEBANON

Lebanon's cedar trees, *above*, were famous in the ancient world. Even the Old Testament of the Bible mentions the fragrant trees. The Temple of Solomon, built in Jerusalem (in modern-day Israel) in the 900s B.C., was made of Lebanese cedar wood. The Egyptians and other ancient peoples also made sarcophagi (coffins), boats, palaces, and other structures from Lebanese cedar. Modern Lebanon has only a few cedar groves left. Some of the trees are thought to be more than one thousand years old.

An unusual mammal found in Lebanon is the **hyrax.** It is about the size of a house cat. The hyrax looks like a rodent, with a thickset body, brown fur, and short legs. It also has hoofed toes like a horse or deer. Although you wouldn't suspect it by looking, its nearest relative is the elephant.

swallows, buzzards, and golden eagles fly through the valley as well. Terns, ospreys, sandpipers, and finches make their homes at the Palm Islands Reserve off Lebanon's northern coast. The mountains are home to many smaller birds, such as cuckoos and woodpeckers, as well as falcons, kites, and other birds of prey (hunting birds). Insects, especially occasional swarms of grasshoppers, are common in Lebanon. Eels, bass, and mullets are among the fish found in Lebanon's rivers. Turtles, seals, and other marine species live in the waters off Lebanon's coast.

Environmental Issues

In the twentieth century, Lebanon became more industrialized, and its environment suffered as a result. Trees were cut for timber and firewood and to make way for roads, buildings, and farmland. This deforestation—destruction of forests—led to other environmental problems. For one thing, when forests are cut down, the plants and animals that normally make their homes there have fewer places to live. Once-common species begin to die out. In addition, cutting large stands of trees leaves hillsides bare and lifeless. Without tree roots to hold the soil in place, soil washes away in the rain and blows away in the wind, a problem known as erosion.

Pollution is another serious problem in Lebanon. Pesticides—chemicals used to kill insects that harm crops—have run off from farmland, polluting rivers and lakes. People have dumped garbage from homes, mines, and factories into rivers, valleys, and landfills. They have dumped oil, sewage, and wastewater into rivers and the sea. Smoke from cars and industry has also polluted the air, especially in Beirut, Lebanon's capital and biggest city.

The Lebanese people have set out to combat some of these problems. The government's Ministry of the Environment is in charge of protecting natural areas and trying to prevent and clean up pollution. Some private groups are also working to protect the environment. These efforts include reforestation—the planting of new trees, such as cedars, oaks, maples, and junipers, to replace those that have been cut down. The government has also signed several international treaties aimed at reducing pollution and keeping natural areas clean.

Throughout the country, the government has set up thirty-one parks and preserves—areas that are off limits to hunting, logging, and development. The largest of these areas is the Chouf Cedar Reserve, which covers about 5 percent of the country's land area. Established in 1996, it holds six cedar forests and great numbers of plants and animals. The Horsh Ehden Nature Reserve, located in the northern part of the Lebanon Mountains, serves as a home for rare birds, butterflies, and wildflowers. The Palm Islands Reserve is made up of several islands off Lebanon's northern coast. It covers about 2 square miles (5 sq. km) of both land and sea. Birds, turtles, and other marine animals make their homes there.

Natural Resources

A small country, Lebanon doesn't have extensive natural resources. However, it has some mineral deposits, including limestone, lignite, iron ore, and sand, all of which are used in building and manufacturing. Salt is mined in Lebanon as well.

Farmland is perhaps Lebanon's most important natural resource. More than 17 percent of the nation's land area is suitable for farming. Important crops include apples, grapes, citrus fruits, olives, vegetables, and tobacco. Many farmers raise livestock such as poultry, goats, sheep, and cattle.

Compared to other nations in the dry Middle East, Lebanon has an abundance of water. Its rivers and springs provide water for household use as well as farming. Dams on the Litani River also create hydroelectricity (electricity produced by the power of rushing water).

Cities

Lebanon's population is estimated at about 3.7 million. Most of these people—about 80 percent—live in urban areas. Most major cities, including Beirut, Tripoli, and Sidon, are located along the seacoast. Zahlé is located inland, in the Bekaa Valley.

BEIRUT Rising on the hilly coast against the background of the Lebanon Mountains, Beirut is Lebanon's capital and largest city. Its population is estimated at 1.2 million people, about one-third of the country's population. Excavations reveal that the Canaanites, the earliest-known inhabitants of Lebanon, were living in Beirut as early as 1900 B.C. Over the centuries, the city grew in size and importance. By the first century B.C., Beirut was the biggest city in Lebanon.

With its coastal location, ancient Beirut was an important center for seagoing trade and exploration. It was also a religious, legal, and educational center. Each ruling empire left its stamp on the city in the form of monuments, roads, and public buildings. Even in modern times, remains of the Greek, Roman, Arab, Ottoman, and other empires can still be seen there.

The city prospered in the late 1800s. People flooded there from other parts of Lebanon, from other Middle Eastern cities, and from Europe. Businesses, such as the silk trade, boomed. The Syrian Protestant College was founded in the city in 1866. It later became known as the American University of Beirut, one of the most highly regarded schools in the Middle East.

After independence in 1943, Beirut emerged as a center for banking, commerce, manufacturing, and tourism. With its beachfront hotels and sidewalk cafés, it was nicknamed the Paris of the Middle East. In the 1970s, however, civil war took its toll on Beirut and other cities in Lebanon. During the war, Beirut was divided into a Christian eastern section and a Muslim western portion. The area in between, called the Green Line, was a barren strip of war-damaged homes and buildings. Shells, bombs, and gunfire destroyed many of the city's grand old buildings. Thousands of city dwellers were killed in the fighting. Others fled their homes.

With the civil war over, modern Beirut has recovered from the devastation. War-damaged buildings have been restored or torn down. New fashionable restaurants, nightclubs, and shops have

Though heavily damaged by civil war in the 1970s and 1980s, **modern Beirut** is recovering well. Find links to more information about Lebanon's cities and smaller communities at www.vgsbooks.com

opened, and the city has come back to life. Visitors to Beirut can enjoy a number of interesting attractions, most notably the famous National Museum, which traces roughly six thousand years of Lebanese history.

TRIPOLI With about 240,000 inhabitants, Tripoli is the second largest city in Lebanon. Located on Lebanon's northern coast, it was settled as early as 1400 B.C. An important seaport, its name was Kadytis in Phoenician times. As the city grew, it developed three distinct sections, which led to the Greek name Tripoli, meaning "three cities." Like Beirut to the south, Tripoli was conquered and reconquered many times, as successive empires took control of Lebanon and the surrounding region.

Modern Tripoli consists of the port district of al-Mina, which sits on a small peninsula, and the city proper, which lies 2 miles (3 km) inland. The Abu Ali, a river that enters the sea east of al-Mina, divides the city east and west. Tripoli remains an important seaport. Some of the city's most fascinating sites are medieval mosques (Islamic houses of worship) dating to the fourteenth and fifteenth centuries.

SIDON Dating back six thousand years, Sidon is one of the oldest cities in Lebanon. During the Phoenician era, it was a great commercial center. Much of its wealth came from murex, a sea animal that produced a valuable purple dye. The dye was traded throughout the ancient world. Over the centuries, conquering nations created many grand buildings in Sidon, including the Sea Castle and the Castle of Saint Louis, both built by Christian invaders in the thirteenth century. Modern Sidon saw extensive fighting during the civil war. In the early 2000s, it is a mid-sized city with about 110,000 people. Many Palestinian refugees from nearby Israel make their homes there.

SHOPPING AT THE SOUK

Souks, or open-air markets, are a standard feature in most Middle Eastern cities, and Lebanese cities are no exception. Most souks feature a maze of twisting alleyways, crowds of shoppers, and vendors selling goods from covered stalls. In Lebanon these markets are great places to buy pastries, herbs, spices, and other foods, as well as handmade jewelry, pottery, glassware, soap, and clothing. Many Lebanese souks date to medieval times.

A souk stall in Beirut overflows with fruits and vegetables.

TYRE The southernmost big city in Lebanon, Tyre is built on a small, rocky outcropping of land that was an island in ancient times. The city's origins date to approximately 2750 B.C. King Hiram, who ruled the city in the 900s B.C., used dirt to create a causeway, connecting the island to the mainland and expanding the city's borders. Like other Lebanese cities, Tyre contains palaces, temples, mosaics, and monuments built by various conquering groups. Because of its southern location, near the Israeli border, Tyre witnessed heavy fighting during the civil war. Modern-day Tyre has approximately 60,000 people. It has Ottoman-era souks (open-air markets), extensive archaeological ruins, and a bustling harbor filled with colorful fishing boats.

ZAHLÉ, with 55,000 people, is the only major Lebanese city not located on the coast. It sits in the near center of the country, about 50 miles (80 km) east of Beirut in the Bekaa Valley. The flourishing resort and market city is known for its open-air restaurants, vineyards, and cascading mountain streams. In the surrounding countryside, visitors can explore Roman ruins. The city itself contains many Ottoman-era houses, dating from the 1500s to the 1900s.

HISTORY AND GOVERNMENT

Lebanon's history dates back thousands of years. In fact, archaeologists have found evidence of prehistoric settlements in the north dating to 5000 B.C. The region's first known inhabitants were the Canaanites, an ancient group mentioned in the Bible. The Phoenicians, probably related to the Canaanites, arrived in the area about 2500 B.C. They occupied the coastal regions of present-day Lebanon, Syria, and northern Israel. This whole region came to be called Phoenicia. On its eastern flank were the Lebanon Mountains and to the west lay the Mediterranean Sea.

By about 1500 B.C., the Phoenicians had built a number of independent cities, including Byblos, Sidon, Tyre, and Beirut, along the Mediterranean seacoast. These cities hosted traders from Egypt and other ancient nations. The major cities fought with one another, but none was strong enough to subdue the others. No leader ever united the cities into one nation. This lack of unity made the Phoenicians vulnerable to foreign conquerors.

Egypt Takes Control

For hundreds of years, the Phoenicians traded with the Egyptians, based nearby on the southeastern edge of the Mediterranean Sea. The Egyptians had great riches, such as gold and other precious metals. But few trees grew in their kingdom, so the Egyptians were happy to trade their gold and metalwork for aromatic Lebanese cedar trees. Egyptian craftspeople fashioned the precious wood into furniture, coffins, and other items.

At the beginning of the sixteenth century B.C., the Hyksos, warlike invaders from central Asia, conquered both Phoenicia and Egypt. But the Egyptians fought back and overtook the Hyksos in the early fifteenth century B.C. The Egyptians then expanded their kingdom to include Phoenicia and other Middle Eastern lands. Conflict continued as the Hittites, a people from Asia Minor (modern-day mainland Turkey), conquered Phoenicia in the mid-1200s B.C. The ruling Egyptians forced the Hittites out a century later, taking Phoenicia

LITERARY ROOTS

The Lebanese town of Byblos takes its name from the papyrus plant. In ancient times, papyrus was used to make paper, and Byblos was a hub of the papyrus trade. Ships carrying papyrus from Egypt would regularly stop at the city on their way to Greece. The Greek word for papyrus was *bublos*, and a variant of this name came to apply to the city. (*Bublos* also meant "book." The English words *bible*, meaning a holy book, and *bibliography*, meaning a list of books, are also derived from *bublos*.) Adding to Byblos's literary heritage, some historians think the Phoenician alphabet originated there.

back into their empire. But Egyptian control soon weakened, leaving the Phoenicians independent by about 1100 B.C.

◎ Travelers and Traders

With independence, the coastal cities of Phoenicia entered a three-hundred-year period of prosperity. During this time, Phoenician craftsmen built fine sailing ships out of cedarwood. They developed the art of navigating the seas, using the stars to guide them to far-off territories.

Phoenician traders carried their nation's lumber, fruits, perfumes, glass, pottery, and metalwork to places around the Mediterranean Sea. In return, the traders brought silver, gold, tin, linen, and other valuable goods from foreign countries back to Phoenicia. One of the Phoenicians' most sought-after trading items was a purple dye, made from the murex, a kind of mollusk. Royalty throughout Asia, Africa, and Europe prized the dye, which they used to make striking purple garments. Many Phoenician merchants grew rich producing and selling purple dye to foreign rulers.

The Phoenicians also established colonies, or settlements, around the Mediterranean region. They colonized parts of the islands of Cyprus and Rhodes near present-day Turkey. They also founded Tarshish, a colony on the coast of Spain, and Carthage in North Africa. They navigated the Red Sea and the Indian Ocean, traveling as far as India. Some historians think they might have sailed all the way around Africa. Others think they sailed up the coast of the Atlantic Ocean to England.

The name Phoenicia comes from the Greek word *phoinikies*, meaning "purple." The name stems from the purple dye the Phoenicians made from mollusks and traded around the world.

Perhaps the most important and lasting Phoenician contribution was their development of a twenty-two-letter alphabet, begun during this era of independence. The Phoenicians used this alphabet to keep business records and to communicate with foreign merchants. Eventually, the alphabet spread to the Greeks and Romans. Our modern Roman alphabet is derived from the original Phoenician writing system.

More Foreign Invasions

The Assyrians, people from the northern area of present-day Iraq, ended the Phoenicians' independence. Wanting to control Mediterranean trade themselves, the Assyrians subdued the Phoenicians in the ninth century B.C. Next, the Babylonians (from the southern part of present-day Iraq) conquered Phoenicia, ruling from 612 to 538 B.C. Then came the Persians (from modern Iran), who ruled until 332 B.C., then the Greeks, led by Alexander the Great. Greek rule lasted until 64 B.C., when Rome took over the Middle East. Along with Palestine to the south, Phoenicia became part of the Roman province of Syria.

Alexander the Great sits before a ritual fire the night before a battle. A priest conducts a religious ceremony for the occasion.

The Phoenicians, not a strong military power, rarely resisted these foreign invasions. Instead, they generally cooperated with the new rulers. As each foreign power approached, most Phoenician cities quickly offered tribute, or payment, to the conquering nation. In this way, they tried to assure that the conquerors would not harm them and would let them maintain some independence.

The Roman and Byzantine Eras

Roman rule in the Middle East began in approximately 50 B.C., and the Roman era proved to be very positive for Phoenicia. Its population grew, and its citizens prospered. The Romans established a law school in Beirut, and the city became an important intellectual center. During this time, the region lost much of its Phoenician identity and became more Roman in its intellectual, economic, and cultural outlook. The Phoenicians adopted a Roman style of architecture, building temples, stadiums, bathhouses, streets, and villas based on Roman models.

During the early years of Phoenician history, the Phoenicians had worshipped many gods and goddesses. But in the first century A.D., a new religion developed in nearby Palestine to the south. This religion,

The Phoenicians erected a massive temple to Bacchus, the Roman god of food and festivity, in Baalbek in eastern Lebanon around 150 A.D.

Christianity, was based on the teachings of a man named Jesus. Soon many people in the Middle East had adopted the Christian faith. In Phoenicia, Christian communities developed in Tyre and Sidon.

In the A.D. 300s, the Roman Empire split into eastern and western sections. Soon afterward, the western half lost power in the Mediterranean world. But the eastern half, called Byzantium, continued to control much of the Middle East, including Phoenicia.

Byzantine emperors practiced Christianity and made it the official religion of their empire in A.D. 379. In the fifth century, a group of northern Phoenician Christians broke away from the mainstream Christian church. They still practiced Christianity, but their beliefs differed from accepted church teachings. This group called themselves Maronites, perhaps taking the name from a hermit named Saint Maroun. Emperor Justinian II persecuted the Maronites for their differing views, so they fled to the rugged Lebanon Mountains. Their descendants remained there, living in isolation, for centuries.

Meanwhile, frequent attacks by outsiders weakened the Byzantine Empire. Eventually, in 636, Arab conquerors, based on the Arabian Peninsula between the Red Sea and the Persian Gulf, took control of the Middle East, including Phoenicia.

Arab Control

The new Arab rulers brought many changes to Phoenicia. They brought a new language, Arabic, a new religion, Islam, and, eventually, a new name, Lebanon.

The Islamic religion had been founded on the Arabian Peninsula by the prophet Muhammad in the early 600s. The new religion encouraged conversion (the process of bringing outsiders into the faith) and the conquering of neighboring peoples. After the Arabs took over Lebanon, many Lebanese people converted to Islam. In the Lebanon Mountains, however, the Maronites continued to practice their distinctive version of Christianity.

The name Lebanon comes from *lubnan*, Arabic for "white." The name refers to the color of Lebanon's snowcapped mountains.

Within thirty years of Muhammad's death, Islam split into two sects: the Sunnis and the Shiites. The Shiites believed that only descendants of Muhammad and his family should lead Islam. The Sunnis thought that caliphs, religious leaders unrelated to the prophet, should head Islam.

After a period of struggle, the Umayyads—a Sunni family—gained control of the growing Islamic Empire. They ruled from their base in Damascus, Syria, for about one hundred years. In Lebanon and other

Rising above the **ancient Umayyad city of Aanjar** (in modern-day eastern Lebanon), the remains of the Umayyads' palace may be seen. The Umayyad family ruled a territory including modern Lebanon from A.D. 661 to 750.

parts of the empire, the Umayyads let local leaders keep a certain amount of status and control. Since the Lebanese had always been great shipbuilders and sailors, the Umayyads used the skills of the Lebanese to establish a strong navy.

The Umayyads' power weakened, and another leading Arab family—the Abbasids—took control of Islamic leadership around 750. The Abbasids made their base in Baghdad in present-day Iraq. Under Abbasid leadership, Islam became more widespread in Lebanon and other Middle Eastern nations. Still, the Maronite Christians maintained their religious identity, remaining isolated in the Lebanon Mountains.

Lebanon's economy grew substantially under Arab control. Merchants in coastal cities prospered by shipping glass, textiles, cedarwood, and pottery throughout the Mediterranean area. This period also saw great intellectual growth. Lebanese scholars made advances in philosophy, law, and medicine.

Beginning in the 1100s, Christian soldiers called Crusaders began arriving in the Middle East from Western Europe. To the Crusaders, the Middle East—particularly Jerusalem in modern-day Israel—was the Holy Land, the place where Christianity had begun. They wanted to capture the Holy Land for Christians. In Lebanon, Crusaders captured Tripoli, Beirut, Sidon, and Tyre. They converted a significant portion of the Lebanese population to Christianity and strengthened ties with the Maronites.

Crusaders and Islamic rulers struggled for control of the Middle East until the thirteenth century, when power fell into the hands of the Mamluks—a group of slaves-turned-soldiers who had taken control in Egypt. Originally from central Asia, the Mamluks extended their realm northeastward to include present-day Lebanon and Syria.

○ The Ottoman Era

The Ottomans, another central Asian people, conquered the Middle East and put an end to Mamluk rule in 1517. From their capital in Turkey, the Ottomans paid little attention to Lebanon. They allowed the local Maan family to rule the region.

From their base in the Lebanon Mountains, the Maans extended their power east and west, into the Bekaa Valley and Lebanon's coastal areas. The Maans were Druzes (members of a secretive religious group that had broken off from Islam in the eleventh century). They made alliances with Lebanon's other religious groups, particularly Maronite Christians. Fakhr ad-Din, whose reign began in 1593, was the strongest Maan leader. The Ottomans grew wary of his ambition and growing power. They executed him in 1635.

Later in the century, the Ottomans entrusted another family, the Shihabs, to govern Lebanon. The Shihabs were Sunni Muslims who began their leadership in 1697. Maronite Christians supported the Shihab family, just as they had the Maans. The succeeding years were prosperous and peaceful, and Lebanon's economy and population grew.

A member of the Shihab family named Bashir Shihab II had dreams of Lebanese independence. Allying himself with Egyptian leader Muhammad Ali Pasha, Shihab ousted the Ottomans from Lebanon in 1831. But the Shihab family governed harshly. The new regime increased taxes and forced men to serve in the army. As a result, Maronites and Druzes revolted. In 1840 Ottoman forces, assisted by the British (who wanted to protect their economic interests in the Middle East), expelled Bashir Shihab II from Lebanon. Ottoman control was restored.

Despite earlier alliances, bitter hostilities and violence erupted between Christians and Druzes in the 1840s. In 1842 several European nations suggested dividing Lebanon into a Christian area in the north and a Druze area in the south. The scheme was tried, but it failed because many Druzes lived in the north and many Christians lived in the south. Members of the dominant faith in each area attacked members of the minority religion.

The Ottomans, with the aid of European powers, intervened in the fighting. In 1861 they appointed a Christian governor to run the whole country. They also created a twelve-member council, with representatives from all the nation's religious groups, to assist the governor. This arrangement brought stability and prosperity to the nation. Beirut, particularly, thrived. Universities were opened, including the Syrian Protestant College. Publishing houses flourished. The nation gained a reputation as a commercial, academic, and cultural center, earning the nickname the Pearl of the Orient.

World War I and After

The Ottomans allied themselves with Germany during World War I, which began in Europe in 1914. Although Lebanon was far from any battles during the war, the conflict disrupted its trade with Western Europe, and its economy suffered drastically. In addition, the ruling Ottomans cut down much of Lebanon's remaining cedar forests, using the wood for fuel.

In this illustration, everyday life in Sidon looks peaceful. The first half of the nineteenth century was a time of religious and political turmoil in Lebanon. But a period of peace and prosperity arrived in the 1860s.

The war ended with a German (and Ottoman) defeat in 1918. The victorious nations, including Britain and France, had promised independence to Arab nations as a reward for their assistance during the war. Prior to independence, Lebanon was placed under a French mandate, which meant that France would administer Lebanon until the French thought Lebanon was ready to govern itself.

The mandate began in 1920, and the first Lebanese constitution went into effect in 1926. The constitution gave Lebanon partial self-rule. The nation had a Lebanese president and lawmakers but was still overseen by a French commissioner. Under French guidance, the Lebanese economy grew strong once again. The government repaired and extended roads throughout the country and enlarged the port of Beirut. New schools were built, and farming methods were improved.

Visit www.vgsbooks.com for links to websites about the twentieth-century history of Lebanon and the Middle East.

Independence

During World War II (1939–1945), the French government was divided into the Vichy government, which allied itself with Germany, and the Free French, a government-in-exile allied with Great Britain, the Soviet Union, and the United States. The Vichy government tried to maintain control of Lebanon during the war, but in 1941, the Free French and their British allies forced the Vichy troops out. The Free French then declared Lebanon to be an independent nation. But in reality, according to terms written into the Lebanese constitution, France still maintained a lot of control over Lebanese affairs. Many French soldiers remained stationed in Lebanon, and French officials held powerful positions in the Lebanese government.

In 1943 the Lebanese people voted for a parliament, or legislature, which chose Bishara al-Khoury as president. Al-Khoury, a Christian, invited Riad al-Solh, a Muslim, to become prime minister. Angered that France still maintained some control in Lebanon, al-Khoury tried to change the constitution to push the French out. In response, the French briefly tried to withdraw Lebanese independence by suspending (temporarily setting aside) the constitution and arresting some government leaders, including President al-Khoury. Lebanese people rioted, and foreign governments protested so strongly that the French relented, freeing the Lebanese leaders and putting the constitution into effect again.

That same year, al-Khoury and al-Solh worked out an unwritten agreement to guide the new Lebanese government. Called the National Covenant, the agreement divided power between the nation's major religious groups. It said that the president would be a Maronite Christian, the prime minister a Sunni Muslim, and the speaker (manager) of the legislature a Shiite Muslim. Seats in the legislature were divided fairly evenly between Christians and Muslims. The Maronites were given control of the army. The Druzes were also given some governmental power.

World War II ended in 1945. After the war, countries around the world formed a new organization, the United Nations (UN), to promote peace and prevent future warfare. Lebanon became a founding member of the new organization. It also became a member of the newly formed Arab League, an association of Arab nations of the Middle East.

In 1948 Israel established itself as an independent nation on Lebanon's southern border. Created to provide a nation for Jewish people in their ancient homeland, Israel was carved out of a territory called Palestine, home to a large Arab population. Israel's creation met with great resistance from its Arab neighbors, including Lebanon. Surrounding Arab states immediately declared war on the new nation. In the course of the fighting, more than 100,000 Palestinians, mostly Muslims, fled from Palestine into Lebanon, where they soon settled into UN-run refugee camps.

Pan-Arabism

Over the centuries, most Lebanese Christians had become Westernized. That is, they had forged ties to the Christian nations of Europe as well as to the United States. Many spoke French or English and attended European-style schools. Lebanese Muslims, on the other hand, felt more kinship with the Arab world. The two groups became increasingly divided both culturally and politically.

Anti-Western sentiment grew, not just in Lebanon but throughout the Middle East. In the mid-1950s, Gamal Abdel Nasser, president of Egypt, led a movement called Pan-Arabism. With this movement, Nasser hoped to strengthen and unite the Arab nations of the Middle East and to rid the region of Western influences. In Iraq, Pan-Arabist rebels overthrew the pro-Western government in 1958.

Many Lebanese Muslims were drawn to Nasser and the Pan-Arabic cause. They were also angered by their own president, Camille Chamoun, a pro-Western Maronite who consistently sided with Europe and the United States in disagreements with Arab nations. Antigovernment violence began to erupt throughout the country. Fearing a full-scale Muslim rebellion like the one in Iraq, Chamoun asked for help from the United States. In July 1958, several thousand U.S. Marines landed at the port of Beirut and helped restore order. Under Chamoun's more moderate successors, the violence subsided, and Lebanon entered a period of relative calm and economic growth.

In **a 1958 skirmish,** antigovernment forces brace for a fight among the Roman ruins at Baalbek.

Israel and the Palestinians

By the 1960s, the Palestinians who had fled to Lebanon during the Israeli war for independence presented a troubling situation for Lebanon. The majority of them were Muslims, who sided with Lebanon's Pan-Arabism movement. The pro-Western Lebanese government became increasingly wary of the Palestinians and tried to restrict their freedom. Escalating the tension, even more Palestinian refugees arrived in Lebanon during the Six-Day War, fought between Israel and its neighbors in 1967.

The Palestinian refugee camps became hotbeds for Palestinian guerrillas, loosely organized bands of fighters determined to strike out at Israel and to protest its control of Palestinian territory. From their bases in Lebanon, Palestinian fighters launched raids against Israeli targets to the south. In December 1968, Lebanese-based Palestinians attacked an Israeli plane at the airport in Athens, Greece. Israeli commandos struck back, destroying thirteen planes at the Beirut airport—a warning to Lebanon to crack down on the Palestinians.

The Burj al Barajinah **Palestinian refugee camp** is near Beirut. The camp was established in 1948. Palestinians continue to live there.

A **Phalange (Lebanese Maronite) Party youth group** parades at a political rally in Beirut.

The Lebanese government was not happy about guerrilla fighters operating within its borders. It sent its army to subdue the Palestinians, but without much success. A stalemate developed, and in 1969 the two sides entered into the Cairo Agreement, a deal that allowed the Palestinians to continue fighting from Lebanon. The concessions to the Palestinians angered Lebanon's Christian Phalange Party, a powerful Maronite faction.

More Palestinian guerrillas arrived in Lebanon in 1970, this time from Jordan, which also didn't want guerrillas operating within its territory and had expelled them. The newly arrived Palestinians included many members of the Palestine Liberation Organization (PLO), a new group dedicated to the destruction of Israel and the creation of a Palestinian nation. The Lebanese attempted to keep tight control over the PLO, but they had little success. The PLO emerged as a powerful faction in southern Lebanon. It continued to attack Israel across the border, and Israel continued to counterattack.

In October 1973, another Arab-Israeli war broke out when Egypt and Syria attacked Israel on the Jewish holy day of Yom Kippur. Known as the Yom Kippur War, the conflict saw fierce fighting between Syrian and Israeli troops near Lebanon's southeastern frontier. Lebanon did not get directly involved in the war, but PLO fighters in Lebanon continued to attack Israel during the conflict.

Civil War

Lebanon became increasingly splintered. The Phalange Party, composed of Maronite Christians, was a powerful force in the government. A group called the National Movement, made up of Pan-Arabist Muslims, wanted to push the Maronites from power. The National Movement allied itself with the Palestinians. The result was civil war.

As fighting tore the country apart, the central government nearly ceased to operate. Religious subgroups formed their own militias (local armies) to protect themselves and to attack enemies. Christian militias slaughtered Palestinians in refugee camps. Palestinians, Muslims, and Druzes massacred Christians. Some foreign nations supplied the different groups with weapons. The Israelis backed the Christians, for instance.

Beirut was split into a Christian eastern section and a Muslim western section. The area in between, called the Green Line, was a barren strip of war-damaged homes and buildings. Christians controlled the north of Lebanon, while Druze, Muslim, and Palestinian forces held authority in the south. Lebanon's economy collapsed.

A concerned Syria stepped in to stop the fighting, sending about forty thousand troops into Lebanon in 1976. The Arab League also tried to broker a cease-fire and set up a peacekeeping force. But none of these efforts proved effective, and the massacres continued.

Holding a photo of her husband and oldest son, a **Palestinian refugee** in a camp near Beirut indicates that both have been killed in Lebanon's civil war. She has eight surviving children to support. (Five are shown with her.)

An Israeli tank patrols the streets of Beirut as part of Israel's 1982 invasion of Lebanon to stop PLO guerrilla fighters.

Palestinians continued to attack Israel from their bases in southern Lebanon. In response, in March 1978, Israeli troops crossed into Lebanon to destroy PLO bases. The United Nations pressured Israel to withdraw and sent a peacekeeping force to restore order. The UN troops set up a buffer zone 15-miles (24-km) wide between Israel and the PLO. Although Israel withdrew its troops, it left the Christian and pro-Israeli South Lebanon Army (SLA) to fight the Palestinians.

Farther north, battles continued to rage throughout Lebanon. Cease-fires failed to hold, and thousands were killed. Syria, which had arrived in 1976 to restore order, was by then a full-scale force in the conflict, switching sides several times in the course of the fighting.

On June 6, 1982, Israeli troops invaded Lebanon once again, this time with seventy-five thousand soldiers. Bent on securing enough territory to stop PLO raids, the Israelis pushed through southern Lebanon. About fifteen thousand PLO fighters retreated up to Beirut. The Israelis followed them and laid siege to West Beirut, striking the city with shells and bombs for two months and killing thousands.

In August the United States finally negotiated a cease-fire between the Israelis and the PLO. U.S., French, and Italian forces arrived and kept watch as PLO leaders and troops were allowed to leave Beirut by sea for other Arab nations. The international forces left within two weeks after the PLO's departure.

PLO fighters head for the Beirut port. They are leaving Lebanon for Arab host countries.

Phalange leader Bashir Gemayel was elected president of Lebanon that same August, only to be killed by a bomb at his party headquarters within a month. The day after his death, the Israeli army advanced again into West Beirut. Soon afterward, Phalange fighters, determined to avenge Gemayel's killing, entered Sabra and Shatila, two Palestinian refugee camps near Beirut. The Phalange troops slaughtered about two thousand people, mostly women and children. Some observers claimed that Israeli forces assisted the attackers.

Forces from France, Italy, and the United States returned to Lebanon in an attempt to foster peace. Amin Gemayel, Bashir's brother, was elected president soon afterward. But tension and violence persisted. Palestinian, Israeli, Christian, Druze, Muslim, and Syrian forces kept attacking one another, with certain groups siding with each other and then switching allegiances and fighting against former allies.

U.S. and other peacekeeping forces were also swept up in the hostilities. In April 1983, a bomb shook the U.S. Embassy in Lebanon, leaving sixty-three dead. A few months later, in October, suicide bombings at the U.S. and French military headquarters in Beirut killed 265 U.S. Marines and 56 French soldiers. Shiite Muslims linked to the radical Hezbollah Party took responsibility for the attacks. Hezbollah opposed both the United States and its affiliation with Israel. In 1984 the same group kidnapped several U.S. reporters, killing one of them.

Remaining Israeli forces left Lebanon in 1985, although Israel continued to back the SLA. Sunnis, Shiites, Druzes, Christians, and Palestinians kept fighting throughout 1986, 1987, and 1988. When

Amin Gemayel's term as president expired in September 1988, more chaos ensued. Muslim and Christian politicians could not agree on a new president, so both groups set up rival governments. Street battles between Muslim and Christian militias raged across the Green Line in Beirut.

Members of the Arab League and Lebanese lawmakers met in September 1989, once again hoping to implement a cease-fire. The meeting resulted in an agreement known as the Taif Accord, which attempted to equalize power between Muslims and Christians in the Lebanese government. Despite some initial opposition and the assassination of newly elected president Rene Mouawad, a Christian, the Lebanese parliament adopted the agreement. The Lebanese army took over control of both East and West Beirut, and the militias began to disband. Lebanon was finally at peace for the first time in fifteen years.

A Shaky Peace

In total, the civil war had killed about 150,000 Lebanese citizens, and about 1.5 million people had lost their homes during the fighting. Hundreds of thousands left Lebanon during the war, seeking a more peaceful life in foreign countries. At war's end, the nation's economy lay in ruins.

Factional hatreds had calmed but had not died out entirely. In the early 1990s, Palestinians reestablished some military bases in the south, and violence continued along the southern border with Israel. Old hostilities between Christians and

LEBANON'S "PARTY OF GOD"

Hezbollah, founded in 1982, is a group of Islamic extremists. Its name means "Party of God" in Arabic.

Hezbollah opposes the West, seeks to create a fundamentalist (religiously strict) Islamic state in Lebanon, and vows to defeat Israel. Since the 1983 bombings of U.S. and French targets in Beirut, the group has carried out several other terrorist attacks against U.S. and Jewish targets around the world. Its fighters continue to attack Israel on Lebanon's southern border. Hezbollah operates a television station, al-Manar, which regularly broadcasts anti-American and anti-Israeli messages. According to the U.S. government, both Iran and Syria support Hezbollah with money, weapons, and advisers.

Within Lebanon, Hezbollah is quite popular. In addition to its television station, it runs a network of schools, hospitals, and other social services. It is a valid political party. Its leader, Sheikh Hasan Nasrallah, is well loved, even by many Lebanese Christians.

Muslims simmered and occasionally erupted into bloodshed. Thousands of Syrian troops remained in Lebanon, and Syria dominated Lebanese politics, angering Lebanese people in all political factions.

Still, Lebanon managed a slow and gradual recovery, with regular elections for parliament and president. Under the leadership of Prime Minister Rafiq Hariri, Lebanon borrowed billions of dollars from international lenders. With these funds, damaged buildings were torn down, and new ones were built. The Lebanese army extended government control to most parts of the country. Even a few tourists began to arrive in Lebanon, visiting its warm Mediterranean beaches and alpine ski resorts.

Responding to Hezbollah attacks, Israel once more invaded southern Lebanon in 1996. Fighting continued on and off until May 2000, when Israel again withdrew its forces. In November 1998, Emile Lahoud was elected Lebanon's president. In 2000 Rafiq Hariri was again named prime minister. Although hostilities still festered, the nation appeared to be moving toward peace and stability.

TRAVELER'S WARNING

Although tourism has increased in Lebanon in recent years and most tourist areas are safe, certain parts of the nation are still dangerous. The south, the scene of heavy fighting between Israeli, Palestinian, and other troops during the civil war, is thought to contain more than 100,000 unexploded landmines and other explosives. The explosives are littered throughout the countryside, and visitors to the area are advised not to leave the main roads. Some regions are off-limits to visitors entirely. Go to www .vgsbooks.com for a link to the latest information from the U.S. State Department.

In 2001 the September 11 terrorist attacks in the United States focused widespread negative attention on the Middle East. Al-Qaeda, an Islamic, anti-American terrorist group, had carried out the attacks, killing about three thousand civilians. Al-Qaeda was based in Afghanistan but also operated in other Middle Eastern nations and in Europe.

The United States charged that some al-Qaeda fighters were training and organizing in Lebanon, especially in Palestinian refugee camps. The United States also labeled Lebanon's Hezbollah Party as a terrorist organization and a threat to the United States. U.S. leaders pressured both the Lebanese and Syrian governments (Syria still maintained thousands of troops in Lebanon and held major political influence there) to arrest suspected terrorists within Lebanon. Already a troubled nation, Lebanon (and its Middle Eastern neighbors) thus found itself caught up in a new struggle, this time the U.S. "War on Terror." The outcome of that war remains uncertain.

Government

Lebanon is an independent republic. In a republic, voters elect leaders to govern on their behalf. The nation's governing principles are set down in a constitution, first written in 1926. According to the constitution, all citizens over age twenty-one are required to vote. Voters elect the 128-member national assembly, or parliament, with new elections every four years.

Poor sanitation and poor medical care, makeshift housing, and food shortages make life in Palestinian refugee camps difficult. Many people rely on food shipments from the United Nations. Despite living in Lebanon for more than fifty years in some cases, most Palestinians have not blended into Lebanese society. The government will not grant them citizenship and severely restricts their freedoms. Most Palestinians are Sunni Muslims.

The national assembly elects the Lebanese president, who serves a six-year term and may not be immediately reelected. The president appoints the prime minister and deputy prime minister. The prime minister appoints a thirty-member cabinet, or body of advisers.

According to terms in the National Covenant and the Taif Accord, governmental jobs are split along religious lines: the president must be a Maronite Christian, the prime minister must be a Sunni Muslim, and the speaker of the legislature must be a Shiite Muslim. Cabinet and national assembly members must also belong to different religions, with proportions equal to those of Lebanon's different religious communities.

The Lebanese court system has various levels. Ordinary courts hear criminal and civil cases and appeals. A court called the Constitutional Council rules on the constitutionality (legality) of laws. A Supreme Council hears charges against the president and prime minister. Religious communities also have courts for deciding cases involving marriage, divorce, guardianship, inheritance, and religious matters.

For local governance, Lebanon is divided into six governorates, or districts. These districts are Beirut, Bekaa, North Lebanon, South Lebanon, Mount Lebanon, and Nabatiyah. Each district is headed by a governor.

 Visit www.vgsbooks.com for links to election news and other information about Lebanon's government.

THE PEOPLE

Lebanon's population is about 3.7 million people. The population is growing at a rate of 1.3 percent and is expected to exceed 5 million by 2025. Lebanon's population density is the highest in the Middle East, with 306 people per square mile (118 people per sq. km). About one-third of the nation's people live in Beirut.

○ Ethnic Groups

Most of Lebanon's people—95 percent—are Arabs. This ethnic group originated on the Arabian Peninsula in ancient times. In Lebanon the Arab population is actually a mix of the many different groups that have occupied the land over the centuries, including Egyptians, Greeks, and others. Some of Lebanon's Arab people are Muslims, some are Christians, and some are Druzes.

Lebanon's Arab population includes roughly 200,000 Palestinians. They arrived in Lebanon in three waves—during the Israeli war for independence in 1948; during the Six-Day War in 1967, when Israel

captured additional Palestinian land; and after Jordan expelled groups of Palestinian guerrillas in 1970. Most Palestinians in Lebanon live in refugee camps.

About 4 percent of Lebanon's population is Armenian. This ethnic group fled to Lebanon during World War I, to escape the mass killing of Armenian people in Turkey. Many Armenians live around Borj Hammoud, east of Beirut, and in the town of Aanjar in the Bekaa Valley. The remaining 1 percent of the Lebanese population is made up of small numbers of other ethnic groups, including Africans and Asians.

○ Changing Traditions

Lebanon is an ancient country, and its society is rooted in centuries-old traditions. Well into the twentieth century, many Lebanese people lived much like their ancestors had hundreds of years earlier. Many lived in small rural villages. They grew crops and raised livestock

NEW AND OLD CLOTHES

Most Lebanese people dress much like people in Europe and the United States. In the cities, they wear Western-style clothing such as business suits, skirts, and casual slacks.

But some Lebanese people wear traditional clothing, depending on their religion and heritage. Examples for men include wide, baggy pants called *sherwals*; red, cone-shaped hats called tarbooshes (also called fezzes); and checkered headscarves called kaffiyehs. Some Muslim women still wear chadors or black veils, while Druze women sometimes wear snow-white veils. Long cloaks and dresses are also traditional outfits for both men and women.

on small plots of land. The family was foremost. Often three generations lived together under one roof.

Women's lives—and especially Islamic women's lives—were very restricted. The husband was the unquestioned head of the household. In many Islamic families, women had to wear veils and long robes called chadors, which covered them from head to foot. They were not allowed to travel alone or work outside the home. Fathers arranged marriages for their daughters, and many young women married in their teens.

In the mid-twentieth century, some age-old traditions began to weaken. After independence in 1943, thousands of villagers began to move to Lebanon's big cities, lured by the promise of good jobs. Western influences such as television and automobiles created a more fast-paced lifestyle. French and other foreign workers brought new ideas and attitudes to Lebanon. Finally, civil war disrupted village life throughout the nation. The PLO and other guerrilla fighters threatened rural families. Roads fell under the control of various militias. Farmers couldn't plant, harvest, or transport their crops. Many of the traditions that had held Lebanese society together began to change.

In modern times, four out of five Lebanese people live in urban areas, including the major cities of Beirut, Tripoli, Tyre, and Sidon. Rebuilt since the civil war, Beirut is an ultramodern city filled with high-rises and fancy hotels. Its streets are crowded with pedestrians, cars, and buses. People in Beirut and other big Lebanese cities live much like city dwellers everywhere. They work in professions such as banking, manufacturing, construction, and communications. They enjoy nightclubs, beaches, television shows, and cultural events.

Women's lives have especially changed. Modern Lebanese women are less constrained by ancient traditions than their mothers and grandmothers were. Modern-day families usually allow their daughters to attend school, hold jobs, and choose their own husbands. Especially in urban areas, Lebanese women work in radio, television, medicine, science, and government. Despite these changes, men still dominate Lebanese government, society, and business. Only 27 percent of Lebanese women hold jobs outside the home, and women hold only 2 percent of the seats in Lebanon's parliament.

Health Care

Medical care in Lebanon is fairly good. Most cities and towns have pharmacies (drugstores) and medical clinics. The government runs several programs to help poor people pay for health care. The nation has one doctor for every 600 people, an above-average figure for the Middle East. Most doctors have been trained in foreign countries, many of them in Europe. The American University of Beirut Hospital is a highly regarded facility.

About 95 percent of the country's population has access to safe drinking water. Life expectancy is 66 years for men and 70 years for women. The infant mortality, or death, rate is 26 deaths per 1,000 births. The maternal mortality rate (numbers of women who die in or around the time of childbirth) is 3 per 1,000. While not as good as Western rates, these figures reflect a decent level of health care in Lebanon, especially when compared to some other Middle Eastern countries.

An ambulance in Amyun waits for action near a hospital.

About 65 percent of married women use contraception, or birth control. The Lebanon Family Planning Association works with the Lebanese government to teach women about birth control and to provide health care to women. Abortion is illegal in Lebanon, except to save the life of the mother. The typical Lebanese woman will have about two children in her lifetime.

The reported rate of human immunodeficiency virus (HIV) is low, at 0.1 percent. HIV is the virus that causes acquired immunodeficiency syndrome, or AIDS. In the 1990s, the Lebanon Family Planning Association and other organizations established programs to teach young people about HIV prevention, including condom use, which helps prevent the sexual spread of HIV. In 2001 Lebanon's Ministry of Health reported only 613 cases of AIDS and HIV infection since 1985. However, health experts think that the real figure might be much higher, and they worry that infection rates might increase.

To learn more about the population statistics, health, and education of Lebanese people, go to www.vgsbooks.com for links.

Education

Lebanon has been an intellectual center of the Arab world for centuries. As early as the third century A.D., Beirut had a law school rivaling the best in the ancient world. In 1866 Protestant missionaries founded the Syrian Protestant College (later the American University of Beirut), one of the top schools in the Middle East. The school was damaged and closed on and off during the civil war, but it reopened in 1991. Saint Joseph's University, founded by Roman Catholics in 1875, has schools of engineering and medicine, as well as a special institute dedicated to Middle Eastern studies. The Lebanese University, also in Beirut, offers programs in law, political science, and the arts. In total, Lebanon has twenty-three universities and colleges. It also has many vocational schools, where students can learn job skills.

Lebanese children must attend primary school for five years (ages six to eleven). Secondary school (middle school and high school) lasts seven years. Enrollment in secondary school is not mandatory, however, so not all children attend. Instead, some Lebanese teenagers take jobs to help support their families. In addition, most of Lebanon's secondary schools are privately run—families must pay to send their children there. Most poor families can't afford the schools. Nevertheless, more than 50 percent of Lebanese students attend private schools, including religious schools called *madrassas*.

Shade trees fill **a courtyard on the American University's Beirut campus.** An annual total of 5,700 students attend classes at the university's campuses in Beirut, Byblos, and Sidon.

Arabic is the language of instruction in all Lebanese schools. The curriculum includes math, science, civics, history, language, and geography. Most students also learn French, English, or both. Lebanon boasts the highest literacy rate in the Middle East—93 percent of men and 82 percent of women can read and write.

CULTURAL LIFE

Lebanon has a rich religious heritage. Yet religion has also been a source of great hatred and violence in Lebanon. Each of Lebanon's major religious groups has subgroups. The subgroups have sometimes formed militias and made alliances over the years, often switching alliances and then fighting those with whom they previously had ties.

More than 60 percent of Lebanon's citizens are Muslims. Muslims follow the Islamic faith. Islam's holy book is the Quran. Begun in the seventh century by the prophet Muhammad, Islam has two main sects—Sunnis and Shiites. The sects developed after Muhammad's death, stemming from a disagreement about how leadership within Islam would be determined. In modern times, the divide between Sunnis and Shiites involves additional factors. For instance, Lebanon's Sunni Muslims tend to be more economically successful than its Shiite Muslims, and Sunnis have more political power. Many Shiites are low-income farmers or laborers. They often see themselves as underprivileged and oppressed, although Shiites slightly outnumber Sunnis in Lebanon.

Approximately 30 percent of Lebanon's people are Christians. Christianity is based on the teachings of Jesus, a spiritual leader who, in the first century A.D., lived in what became modern-day Israel. Lebanon's Christians are split among several different churches: Greek Orthodox, Armenian Orthodox, Catholic, and Protestant. Most belong to a sect called Maronite.

The Maronites originated in Syria in the fourth century A.D. Although they practiced Christianity, they adopted ideas about Jesus' divine (godly) and human aspects that differed from accepted Christian teachings. The larger Christian church condemned the Maronites for their beliefs. In the seventh century, they retreated into remote parts of the Lebanon Mountains to practice their faith freely. In the twelfth century, when European Crusaders arrived in the Middle East, the Maronites reestablished ties with the mainstream Christian church.

Modern-day Maronites live in towns and cities throughout Lebanon, with heavy concentrations in the Mount Lebanon district and East Beirut. They are a powerful political group. The National Covenant states that Lebanon's president must be a Maronite Christian.

Roughly 7 percent of Lebanon's citizens are Druze. The Druze are a fiercely independent and secretive religious group that split off from the Shiite Muslims in the eleventh century. Their first leader was al-Hakim bi Amrillah, said to be the incarnation (earthly presence) of God.

The Druze follow several basic practices, including dealing with one another truthfully, renunciation of other religions, belief in al-Hakim as a godly presence, and submission to God's will. They also believe in reincarnation (rebirth after death) and that al-Hakim will someday reappear, take over the world, and establish justice. The Druze gather for prayer on Thursday evenings. Outsiders are not allowed to attend their worship services.

Druze women (in white veils), men, and youths attend a worship service.

The **Phoenician alphabet,** as inscribed on this rock, was much simpler than earlier writing systems because it assigned a symbol (a letter) to each sound, with just twenty-two letters in all. Other ancient writing systems, such as Egyptian hieroglyphics, assigned different symbols to whole words or ideas—so writers had to learn thousands of symbols to use the systems.

Language and Literature

The Phoenicians, one of Lebanon's earliest peoples, are remembered in part for their twenty-two-letter alphabet, which became the basis for our modern Roman alphabet. The Phoenicians carried their alphabet with them as they traded and traveled throughout the Mediterranean world. The Greeks adopted the system, and then the Romans and other European peoples adopted it.

The Phoenician language was a variant of Semitic, related to Hebrew and other ancient Middle Eastern languages. Later on, in the first century A.D., people in Phoenicia began to speak Aramaic, another Semitic language. Finally, Arab conquerors spread Arabic throughout the Middle East, including Lebanon.

In modern times, Arabic is the official language of Lebanon, although some people also speak French, English, or Armenian. The Arabic alphabet has twenty-eight letters. Written with small dots, tight curlicues, and wavy and curved lines, these letters do not look anything like the letters developed by the Phoenicians or used by modern English speakers.

Lebanon, especially Beirut, has long been a center of learning and literature—dating to Roman times and earlier. A thriving publishing industry developed in the city in the nineteenth century. Beirut's most

Kahlil Gibran's work includes paintings and drawings, such as his self portrait *(right)*. But he is a famous Lebanese poet too. Read more about Gibran and other famous Lebanese writers and artists. Go to www.vgsbooks.com for links.

Lebanon's publishing industry dates to the nineteenth century, and it is still strong there. In fact, about 70 percent of the books and other literature published in the Middle East are produced in Lebanon.

famous writer was a nineteenth-century poet, novelist, and painter named Kahlil Gibran. His most well-known work is *The Prophet,* a long poem about love. Other, more recent books have examined the civil war. Examples include Etel Adnan's *Sitt Marie Rose,* Tawfiq Yusuf Awwad's *Death in Beirut,* and Hanan al-Shaykh's *Story of Zahra.*

Performing Arts

Visitors to Lebanon will hear lots of music, especially at the nation's many arts festivals. Singers are especially popular. Traditional Lebanese songs (and other Middle Eastern songs) are often slow, rich, and dreamy. Orchestras accompany the singers with equally dreamy background music. The orchestras usually feature Western-style instruments such as violins and clarinets, along with traditional Middle Eastern instruments such as the tabla, a kind of drum, and the oud, a stringed instrument that resembles a lute. Some Lebanese musicians have combined traditional musical styles with more modern styles such as pop and jazz. The most famous Lebanese singer is Fairouz, noted for her silky smooth voice.

Dance is also commonplace in Lebanon. At weddings and other celebrations, people usually dance the *dabke,* an old-style folk dance. Participants dance in a circle, with their hands joined. Belly dancing, featuring female dancers with swirling hips and sparkly costumes, is commonly performed in Lebanese nightclubs and restaurants, as well as at weddings. A well-known troupe called Caracalla performs traditional and modern dances at Lebanese festivals and other events. Lebanon also has a small theater scene, based largely in Beirut.

Art and Architecture

Lebanese craftspeople have been creating intricate glassware, jewelry, leather goods, and other wares since ancient times. Some craftspeople still carry on these traditions. In the souks of Sidon, Tripoli, and other cities, shoppers can buy old-style pottery, copper goods, and other handcrafted items. Lebanon's Palestinian refugees are acclaimed for their beautiful embroidery work. Jazzin, a town in the Chouf Mountains, is famed for the crafting of knives with delicate animal-bone handles.

The fine arts thrive in Lebanon as well. Kahlil Gibran, most famous as a writer, was also a talented painter. Another well-known painter was Omar Onsi. The Lebanon Academy of Fine Arts was established in 1937 in Beirut. Galleries and museums followed.

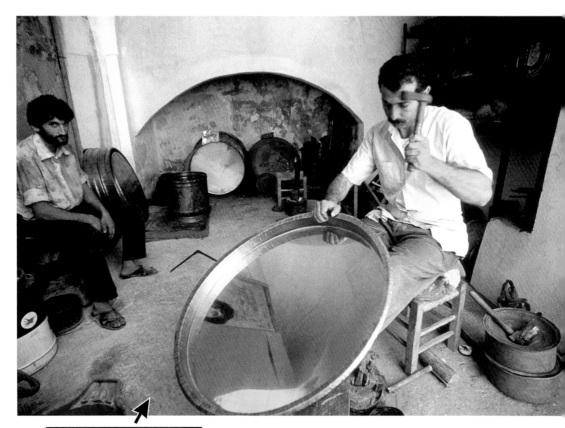

An artist in a souk in Tripoli hammers a copper platter into shape.

Soon Beirut had a lively visual arts scene, contributing to its "Paris of the Middle East" reputation. Arts activity halted during the civil war, but the arts scene has since been revived. Contemporary painters (including the brother and sister Fulvio and Flavia Codsi), sculptors (most notably Salwa Raodash Shkheir), and other visual artists are again hard at work in the nation's cities.

Anyone interested in the history of architecture will find Lebanon a virtual classroom. Its towns and cities hold structures dating back thousands of years, to the days of the nation's earliest human inhabitants. Temples, monuments, and carvings from the Phoenician, Greek, Roman, Arab, Crusader, Ottoman, and French-mandate eras still stand—some of them in ruins, some standing next to newly built skyscrapers and high-rise apartments. Famous examples include the Phoenician-era Obelisk Temple at Byblos; the Roman-era Temple of Jupiter in Baalbek; Crusader-era castles in Tripoli, Byblos, and Sidon; and the Ottoman-era Grand Seraglio (sultan's palace) in Beirut. Unfortunately, especially in Beirut, many historic buildings

The **Phoenician-era Obelisk Temple in Byblos** was built more than three thousand years ago.

were damaged or destroyed in the civil war.

Modern Media

About fifteen newspapers are published regularly in Lebanon. Most are published in Arabic, but some are written in English or French. Fifteen television and more than forty radio stations broadcast in Lebanon as well. The radio and television shows offer a variety of news, entertainment, sports, and other programming, some of it in English and French.

Telephone lines and other communication services were badly damaged during the civil war, but the lines have since been restored. By the 2000s, about 700,000 Lebanese households had landline telephone service, and a growing number of people (580,000) had cell phones. About fifteen Internet service providers operate in Lebanon, and most cities have cybercafes. About 300,000 Lebanese customers have Internet access, a figure that appears to be growing quickly.

Movies are a popular pastime in Lebanon. Most towns have at least one theater, generally showing Hollywood movies, usually with Arabic subtitles. Lebanon also has an impressive film industry of its own, including four film schools. Many Lebanese filmmakers specialize in documentary (nonfiction) films. Jocelyn Saab's *Once upon a Time in Beirut*, Ziad Duweyri's *West Beirut*, and Mai Masri's *Children of Shatila* are all documentary films that deal with the civil war.

Foods of Lebanon

Lebanon has a rich culinary tradition, combining Middle Eastern, Turkish, and French influences. Many dishes are spicy, and all are tasty.

A meze, a Lebanese buffet, is a big selection of hot and cold appetizers: spicy salads, mashed beans mixed with olive oil, zesty

PARIS OF THE MIDDLE EAST

Lebanon has long been known as the Pearl of the Middle East. Beirut has experienced a cultural rebirth since the civil war. International trendsetters have lately been flocking to Beirut's fashionable nightclubs, restaurants, and hotels. In the early 2000s, *Newsweek* magazine called Beirut one of the world's top twelve "Capitals of Style." It shared the honor with Paris, Los Angeles, Rio de Janeiro, and Tokyo.

To read more about the arts, music, and mass media such as radio, television, and the Internet in Lebanon, go to www.vgsbooks.com for links.

STUFFED TOMATOES/ BANADOURA MAHSHI

Stuffed vegetables are very popular in Lebanon and are served as part of a meze or as a main course.

4 large, ripe tomatoes

½ lb. lean ground lamb or beef

¼ c. pine nuts

1 tsp. salt

¼ tsp. pepper

¼ tsp. ground ginger

½ tsp. cinnamon

¼ tsp. allspice

¼ tsp. ground cumin

1 14½-oz. can crushed tomatoes

⅔ c. water

1. Preheat oven to 350°F. Grease a 9×9-inch baking dish.
2. Cut tops off tomatoes. Using a spoon, carefully scoop out pulp, making sure not to tear the skins. Save tops and pulp.
3. Place tomatoes in baking dish.
4. In a large skillet, cook meat over medium-high heat until brown, stirring to break into small pieces. Remove meat from skillet with a slotted spoon and place in a medium bowl. Save the grease.
5. Add pine nuts to grease from the meat and sauté over medium-high heat 2 to 3 minutes, or until lightly browned.
6. Remove pine nuts from skillet with a slotted spoon and stir into browned meat. Add spices and mix well.
7. Place pulp from tomatoes in a fine sieve and place sieve over the bowl containing the meat mixture. With the back of a spoon, force pulp through sieve into the bowl.
8. Spoon meat mixture into hollowed-out tomatoes. Replace tops on tomatoes.
9. Pour crushed tomatoes over tops of stuffed tomatoes. Add the water to bottom of baking dish.
10. Bake uncovered for 20 to 30 minutes. Serve hot.

Serves 4

meatballs with nuts, tabbouleh (chopped tomatoes, scallions, parsley, and cracked wheat), and stuffed grape leaves, just to name a few. Lamb is a popular main dish. It's almost always served with rice. Kibbe—a paste of lamb and bulgur wheat—is Lebanon's national dish. Shish kebab is another well-loved dish consisting of skewered cubes of lamb, green peppers, and onions. For a quick lunch (bought from a street vendor, perhaps) many people like to eat *shwarma*—grilled lamb or chicken—inside a piece of *khobz*, or Lebanese flatbread. Lebanese desserts include baklava, a flaky pastry filled with chopped nuts and honey, and halvah, squares of fruit and nuts covered with a sweet sesame paste. Lebanese people like to drink strong, sweet coffee. Other favorite drinks are sweet tea, fresh juices, and lemonade. *Ayran*, a salty yogurt drink, is also popular. Lebanon produces its own wine, at wineries located throughout the Bekaa Valley. Arrack, a strong brandy, is another widespread favorite.

In an open-air souk in Tripoli, a cook is **making shish kebab** for customers.

In a **Maronite procession, or parade, in honor of Saint Aquilina,** men carry a painting of her through the streets of Jubayl.

Holidays and Festivals

Lebanon observes many holidays throughout the year. Some holidays are secular, or nonreligious. These include New Year's Day (January 1), Labor Day (May 1), and Independence Day (November 22). With its various religious groups, it's not surprising that Lebanon also celebrates many religious holidays. Maronites observe the Feast of Saint Maroun, their patron saint (protector), on February 9. All Lebanese Christians observe Easter in March or April and Christmas on December 25.

Muslims also observe a number of holidays, including the Islamic new year, Muhammad's birthday, Eid al-Fitr (the Feast of Fast Breaking, held at the end of the holy month of Ramadan), and Eid al-Adha (the Feast of Sacrifice, when people give food to the poor). Islam uses the lunar calendar (based on the cycles of the moon), which is different from the Gregorian calendar used in the United States and many other countries. Therefore, according to the Gregorian calendar, Islamic holidays occur at different times each year.

Performing arts festivals are well-loved events for people of all faiths and backgrounds. Most cities and many small towns host a festival every year. Many are held against a backdrop of dramatic ancient ruins. The most famous is the Baalbek Festival, established in 1956. World-renowned dancers, singers, and musicians have performed there over the years, with Baalbek's famous Roman-era temples lit up behind them. Other well-known festivals take place in Byblos, Tyre, and Beirut. Most festivals feature classical, jazz, or popular music—or a combination of all three.

Sports and Recreation

Lebanese people love watching soccer and rooting for local teams. Local basketball games also draw lots of fans. Horse racing and auto racing are very popular with Lebanese spectators as well.

Those who like to take part in sports themselves have plenty of choices in Lebanon. The country has terrific downhill ski slopes in the Lebanon Mountains. It has a warm, sunny coastline, perfect for snorkeling, waterskiing, windsurfing, and sailing. Inland, people can raft or kayak on rivers or trek through one of several nature preserves. Many visitors who come to Lebanon spend time enjoying its natural wonders.

THE ECONOMY

With its numerous ports on the Mediterranean Sea, Lebanon has long been a commercial center—dating back to the days of the Phoenician traders. What's more, Lebanon sits at the crossroads of three continents: Asia, Africa, and Europe. As a result, its port cities have long welcomed traders and travelers from all over the world.

In the nineteenth and twentieth centuries, Lebanon became a center for new industries, notably banking and publishing. After independence, the nation developed a strong economy, a stable currency (money that retained its value), and thriving industries. The country produced abundant electric power from its hydroelectric plants. It had a well-maintained highway system and large, modern seaports and airports. International tourists flocked to Lebanon to visit its famous ancient sites, magical cedar trees, and downhill ski resorts.

The civil war, however, all but destroyed the Lebanese economy. Bullets, bombs, and shells damaged the nation's roads, buildings, ports, and power facilities. In turmoil and unable to collect taxes, the

government went bankrupt. Inflation (rising prices) soared, and the value of Lebanese money declined drastically. Because of violence in the countryside, farmers were unable to get their goods to market. Foreign businesses closed their offices in Beirut and other cities, fearing for the safety of their employees. Tourists no longer wanted to visit Lebanon. Millions of citizens left the country during the war, moving to foreign nations in search of peace and employment.

After the war, Prime Minister Rafiq Hariri undertook an ambitious rebuilding program, named Horizon 2000. A rich businessman, Hariri secured more than $18 billion in loans from banks and foreign countries. With this money, the Lebanese government repaired roads, ports, power lines, communications systems, and buildings that had been damaged by war. The economy recovered greatly in the early 1990s, then slowed somewhat in the late 1990s.

In the early 2000s, the Lebanese economy is stable but slow. Many problems remain. For example, the nation's unemployment rate is high, at more than 14 percent. The Lebanese government has classified 28 percent of the nation's people as poor. The government must spend a great deal of its money paying back loans it took out in the 1990s, which cuts into funding for schools, hospitals, and other social programs. Despite these obstacles, the economy shows signs of promise. Foreign businesses have returned to Lebanon. U.S. companies such as Microsoft, Coca-Cola, FedEx, and General Electric have branch offices there. Tourism has picked up too. And certain industries—especially banking—are strong and growing.

Services

The service sector—including banking, insurance, trade, publishing, tourism, health care, and education—is the largest portion of Lebanon's economy. It accounts for 67 percent of the nation's gross domestic product (GDP), the total value of all goods and services produced in the country in one year.

Based in Beirut, the nation's banking industry is particularly prosperous, with a good reputation worldwide. More than one hundred foreign and domestic (Lebanese) banks operate throughout the nation. A stock exchange is located in Beirut.

Some **banks in Beirut** compete for business from the same building. Beirut's strong banking industry has helped its economic recovery. Go to www.vgsbooks.com for links to news about Lebanon's economy.

CHILDREN AT WORK

Many people in Lebanon are poor, and many Lebanese children must work to help support their families. According to the United Nations, more than 10 percent of Lebanese children ages 14 to 17 have some kind of job. They labor in a variety of different workplaces, including factories, restaurants, construction sites, stores, and farms.

A youth in a Palestinian refugee camp near Beirut tries to sell a pair of chickens.

Lebanon still does a lot of international trade. It exports fruits, vegetables, tobacco, textiles, metal products, paper products, and jewelry, primarily to France, Switzerland, the United States, and other Middle Eastern nations. Lebanon imports food, vehicles, minerals, chemicals, textiles, and fuel such as petroleum. Its primary import partners are Italy, France, Germany, and the United States. Exports total approximately $1 billion each year and imports total $6 billion annually.

The Lebanese tourism industry has seen a tremendous recovery since the civil war. The famous Casino du Liban (Casino of Lebanon) is a popular tourist destination north of Beirut. It closed during the war but reopened in 1996. Numerous glitzy hotels opened in Beirut in the early 2000s. The nation's six ski resorts welcomed an increasing number of visitors. Tourism accounts for 9 percent of Lebanon's gross domestic product each year, with more than 800,000 visitors annually. Nearly half of the tourists who visit Lebanon come from other Middle Eastern nations.

Industry and Agriculture

Industry is Lebanon's second largest economic sector, accounting for 21 percent of GDP. Lebanese processing plants and factories produce a variety of goods, including textiles, cement, chemicals, electrical products, furniture and other wood products, jewelry, and food products. Other plants make bricks, stone products, plastic, and rubber.

In earlier centuries, Tripoli was a famous soap-making center. Soap makers created their products by hand, using olive oil, honey, animal fats, and natural dyes and fragrances. A few soap makers still operate in Tripoli, mostly selling their products to tourists.

Agriculture is Lebanon's smallest economic sector, totaling 12 percent of GDP. More than 17 percent of Lebanon's land is arable, or suitable for farming. Most crops are grown in the Bekaa Valley, with some farms

Farms checker the landscape of Lebanon's fertile Bekaa Valley.

Lebanon is home to more than 500,000 goats. Large herds frustrate local forest conservationists, however. Alternative pastures such as this meadow are scarce. Most goats live in Lebanon's 200 square miles (518 sq. km) of forests. There they eat tree seedlings and other important plants all year long.

along the Mediterranean coast. The nation's primary agricultural products are citrus fruits, tomatoes, apples, cherries, potatoes, sugar beets, olives, and tobacco. Some farmers grow grapes, which are then made into wine. Other farmers raise sheep and goats. Lebanon also has a small fishing industry along the Mediterranean Sea and a small forestry industry.

Transportation

Roads are Lebanon's main means of transportation. Approximately 4,500 miles (7,240 km) of roads crisscross the country, more than 85 percent of them paved. One major highway runs from Syria in the north, through Lebanon's major coastal cities, to the Israeli border in the south. Another major highway stretches from Beirut through the Lebanon Mountains and the Bekaa Valley, across the Anti-Lebanon

This **highway near Shikka** in northern Lebanon is paved with fresh black asphalt.

Mountains to Damascus, Syria. People travel from town to town in buses or private cars. Taxis and buses operate in all major cities.

The nation has a small railroad system, but it was damaged during the civil war and has not yet been repaired. None of the nation's rivers are navigable (large enough for boat travel). Cargo ships, fishing boats, and passenger vessels travel in and out of the major ports of Beirut, Tripoli, Juniyah, and Sidon. For air transportation, the nation has five airports with paved runways. Beirut International Airport is the largest, with regular flights to cities in Europe, Africa, and Asia.

▶ Future Challenges

Lebanon's people have many reasons to hope. The civil war that ravaged their country in the 1970s and 1980s has come to an end.

Private militias have disbanded, and the nation has been largely peaceful for more than ten years. The government is back in operation, and the economy, although sluggish, shows promising trends.

Yet problems remain. Religious and political differences persist and sometimes erupt into violence. The Palestinians still live in squalid camps. Other Lebanese still struggle with poverty and unemployment. What's more, Lebanon sits in the heart of one of the world's most troubled regions, with violence raging in many neighboring countries.

Some Lebanese people engage in a black market, or illegal, economy, buying and selling goods without government licenses or oversight. Some make copies of books, videos, cassettes, and computer software without permission and then sell them. Others buy and sell dangerous goods such as illegal drugs and weapons.

But Lebanon also has numerous strengths. It boasts a highly educated population, high-quality educational and health-care systems, a strong cultural heritage dating back to ancient times, a strong banking and financial industry, breathtaking natural beauty, and a proud history. If the Lebanese people draw on these assets in the future as they have in the past, their chances for success and prosperity will be high.

Timeline

CA. 3000 B.C. The Canaanites settle in present-day Lebanon.

CA. 2500 B.C. The Phoenicians arrive in the coastal regions of present-day Lebanon. They establish a strong trading relationship with Egypt to the southwest.

CA. 1550 B.C. Egypt expands its empire into the Middle East, including control of Phoenicia.

CA. 1100–842 B.C. The Phoenicians experience a period of independence, establishing colonies and trade routes throughout the ancient world. They also develop a twenty-two-letter alphabet.

842 B.C. The Assyrians conquer Phoenicia.

CA. 800 B.C. Greeks begin to adopt the Phoenician alphabet.

612–538 B.C. The Babylonians rule Phoenicia.

538–332 B.C. The Persians rule Phoenicia.

332 B.C. Alexander the Great, a Greek general, captures the city of Tyre. Phoenicia comes under control of the Greek Empire.

64 B.C. Pompey the Great, a Roman general, conquers Phoenicia. The nation becomes part of the Roman province of Syria.

A.D. 0–100 Christianity develops in Palestine, south of Lebanon.

200s The Romans found a prestigious law school in Beirut.

CA. 395 The Roman Empire splits into eastern and western halves. The eastern half, Byzantium, retains control in Phoenicia and the rest of the Middle East.

400s Maronite Christians split from the main Christian church.

CA. 610 The prophet Muhammad founds Islam on the Arabian Peninsula.

LATE 600s Arab armies conquer the Middle East, including present-day Lebanon.

1100s Crusaders arrive in the Middle East from Europe. In Lebanon they capture Tripoli, Beirut, Sidon, and Tyre. The Maronites reunite with the main Christian church.

LATE 1200s The Mamluks extend their power from Egypt into Lebanon and Syria.

1517 The Ottoman Turks take control of the Middle East.

CA. 1607 Fakhr ad-Din emerges as Lebanon's first national leader.

1831 Bashir Shihab II succeeds in overthrowing Ottoman rule in Lebanon.

1840   The Ottomans take back control of Lebanon.

1866   Protestant missionaries found the Syrian Protestant College.

1918   Germany and its Ottoman allies are defeated in World War I.

1920   Lebanon is placed under a French mandate.

1923   Kahlil Gibran's *The Prophet* is published.

1926   Lebanon drafts its first constitution.

1941   France gives Lebanon partial self-rule.

1943   Lebanon wins full independence from France.

1945   Lebanon becomes a founding member of the United Nations.

1948   Israel declares its independence. More than 100,000 Palestinian refugees flee to Lebanon from the new state of Israel.

1956   The Baalbek Festival holds its first season, with performances by ballet dancer Rudolf Nureyev, jazz great Duke Ellington, singers Joan Baez and Ella Fitzgerald, and others.

1958   U.S. Marines arrive in Lebanon to quell a Muslim rebellion.

1967   Additional Palestinian refugees arrive in Lebanon following the Six-Day War in Israel.

1975   Civil war breaks out in Lebanon, with the formation of Palestinian, Muslim, Christian, and Druze militias.

1978   Israel invades southern Lebanon in response to Palestinian attacks.

1982   Israeli troops attack PLO fighters in West Beirut. Phalange troops slaughter Palestinian civilians in the Sabra and Shatila refugee camps.

1983   A suicide bomber kills more than three hundred U.S. and French peacekeeping troops in Beirut.

1989   Arab leaders create the Taif Accord, equalizing power between Muslims and Christians in the Lebanon government. The civil war ends.

1993   Prime Minister Rafiq Harari initiates Horizon 2000, a plan to rebuild Lebanon's destroyed cities and infrastructure.

2003   Lebanon celebrates sixty years of independence with a parade, a public holiday, and other events.

2004   For the first time in municipal elections, women candidates representing the Hezbollah Party run for public office.

COUNTRY NAME Republic of Lebanon

AREA 4,000 square miles (10,360 sq. km)

MAIN LANDFORMS Coastal Plain, Lebanon Mountains, Bekaa Valley, Anti-Lebanon Mountains

HIGHEST POINT Qurnat as Sawda, 10,115 feet (3,083 m) above sea level

LOWEST POINT Sea level

MAJOR RIVERS Litani, Orontes, Musa, Ibrahim, Awwali

ANIMALS deer, porcupines, badgers, foxes, hares, wolves, wild boars, gazelles, wild goats, hyraxes

CAPITAL CITY Beirut

OTHER MAJOR CITIES Tripoli, Sidon, Tyre, Zahlé

OFFICIAL LANGUAGE Arabic

MONETARY UNIT Lebanese lira (also called the Lebanese pound) 100 piastres = 1 lira

LEBANESE CURRENCY

The Lebanese monetary unit is the Lebanese lira, known also as the Lebanese pound. The lira is divided into 100 piastres. During the civil war, the nation witnessed dramatic inflation, and the value of the lira fell. As a result, one Lebanese lira is worth very little money. In fact, it takes about 1,500 lira to equal just one U.S. dollar. The Lebanese government issues paper bills worth 50, 100, 250, 500, 1,000, 5,000, 10,000, 20,000, 50,000, and 100,000 lira. The government no longer issues piastres, since they are essentially worthless. Almost all Lebanese stores and restaurants accept U.S. dollars in addition to lira.

Currency   Fast Facts

Lebanon's flag consists of three horizontal stripes—a white stripe between two red ones. A cedar tree stands in the center of the white stripe. The two red stripes symbolize the blood of those who died for Lebanon. The white stripe stands for Lebanon's snowcapped mountains. The cedar tree symbolizes immortality and peace. The flag was created in 1943.

Lebanon's national anthem was adopted in 1927. The words were written by Rachid Nakhlé, with music by Wadih Sabra. The song is sung in Arabic. Here is an English translation:

All of us! For our country, for our flag and glory!
Our valor and our writings are the envy of the ages.
Our mountains and our valleys, they bring forth stalwart men.
And to perfection all our efforts we devote.
All of us! For our country, for our flag and glory!

Our elders and our children, they await our country's call,
And on the day of crisis they are as lions of the jungle.
The heart of our east is ever Lebanon,
May God preserve her until the end of time.
All of us! For our country, for our flag and glory!

The gems of the east are her land and sea.
Throughout the world her good deeds flow from pole to pole.
And her name is her glory since time began.
Immortality's symbol—the cedar—is her pride.
All of us! For our country, for our flag and glory!

 You can listen to the Lebanese national anthem. A link is available at www.vgsbooks.com.

SAMIR BANNOUT (b. 1955) Nicknamed the Lion of Lebanon, Bannout earned international fame as a bodybuilder. Bannout was born in Beirut but moved to the United States in 1974. He settled in Detroit, Michigan, where he took up the sport of bodybuilding. He won many championships, including the Mr. Olympia pageant in 1983. Retired from competition, Bannout lives in Los Angeles with his wife and two children.

FAKHR AD-DIN (1572–1635) A member of the Maan family, ad-Din ruled Lebanon during the Ottoman era. Himself a Druze born in Baqlin (near Beirut), he reached out to Maronites in the Lebanon Mountains and united Druze and Maronite factions under his own rule. He gradually expanded his power to include most of Lebanon, Syria, and Palestine. He set out to modernize Lebanese society by developing the nation's silk industry, improving its olive-oil industry, strengthening ties and trading relationships with European nations, and upgrading cities and ports. The Ottomans grew wary of ad-Din's growing power and had him executed in 1635. The country's first nationwide hero, he is considered the father of modern Lebanon.

FAIROUZ (b. 1935) Lebanon's most well-loved singer, Fairouz was born and educated in Beirut. Her name at birth was Nouhad Alboustani. She began performing and making records in the 1950s and soon became famous throughout the Arab and Western world. Noted for her silky voice, Fairouz has sung everything from folk songs to religious music to jazz. In the 1960s, she was a regular performer at the annual music festival in Baalbek. Fairouz lived in Paris during the civil war but returned to Lebanon in 1994. Forty thousand people came to hear her sing in Beirut upon her return. Fairouz's son, Ziad, is also a talented composer and musician.

KAHLIL GIBRAN (1883–1931) Born in the town of Bsharri, Gibran attended primary school in Beirut, then moved to Boston, Massachusetts, with his parents. In 1899 he returned to Beirut, where he studied classical Arabic at a Maronite school. He continued to travel, first back to Boston, where he published his first essays; then to Paris, where he studied painting; then to New York, where he continued to paint and write essays and short stories. Gibran's painting and literary works are said to be "mystical," having dreamlike and spiritual qualities. Many of his works deal with peace, religious tolerance, and love. His most famous work, a long poem called *The Prophet,* was published in 1923. It has been translated into more than twenty languages.

NICHOLAS HAYEK (b. 1928) Beirut-born Hayek is cofounder of SMH, a Swiss watchmaking company that creates Swatch watches, some of the most popular and best-selling watches in the world. The son of a Lebanese mother and an American father, Hayek studied at the International College in Beirut. He later moved to Switzerland, where he worked as a business consultant. Hayek and SMH introduced the colorful and inexpensive Swatch watches in the 1980s, and the product met with immediate success. In 1998 Hayek helped develop the tiny Smart car for the DaimlerChrysler company.

BERNARD KHOURY (b. 1968) Beirut-born Khoury is a world-famous architect. Since the civil war, he has been deeply involved in the rebuilding of Beirut. Many of his buildings there incorporate memories of the war. For instance, his BO18 nightclub was built on the site of a wartime massacre. His Centrale restaurant was built in the shell of a destroyed villa. Khoury studied architecture at the Rhode Island School of Design and Harvard University in the United States. He has taught architecture at Beirut's American University and at other schools around the world. Khoury lives and works in both Beirut and New York.

OMAR ONSI (1901–1969) Impressionist painter Omar Onsi was born in Beirut. As a young man, he entered the Syrian Protestant College. While enrolled in school, Onsi learned the basics of drawing and painting from an artist named Khalil Saleeby. He later moved to Jordan, where he painted many desert scenes, as well as portraits of the Jordanian royal family. He then furthered his study of art in Paris. Returning to the Middle East in 1930, he continued to paint portraits, landscapes, and village life. Usually painted in watercolors or oils, his works capture the spirit of Lebanon's people and the beauty of its natural scenery. They have been exhibited throughout the world.

ELIE SAAB (b. 1964) Born in Beirut, fashion designer Saab has been interested in art and fashion since childhood. He opened his first atelier, or design studio, in Beirut in 1982. He showed off his first collection that same year at the Casino du Liban. He quickly became famous throughout the Middle East and was hired to design clothing for some of the region's most prominent women, including queens and princesses. He soon also had shows and clients throughout Europe. Best known for his evening gowns, Saab has become a favorite of Hollywood stars, including Halle Berry, who often wear his dresses to the Oscar ceremonies. He also runs the ES-MOD fashion school in Beirut.

HANAN AL-SHAYKH (b. 1945) Beirut-born al-Shaykh is a highly acclaimed novelist, short-story writer, and playwright. Many of her works deal with women's lives, relationships, and marriage. Educated at the American College for Girls in Cairo, Egypt, she began her career as a television and magazine journalist. Her first novel was published in 1971. Many of her works, including *Story of Zahra* (1980), *Women of Sand and Myrrh* (1989), *Beirut Blues* (1992), and *Only in London* (2000), have been translated into English. With Lebanon torn apart by civil war, al-Shaykh left her home country in 1976. She moved to Saudi Arabia and then to London.

While most areas in Lebanon of interest to tourists are safe to visit, certain parts of the nation are still dangerous. The south, the scene of heavy fighting between Israeli, Palestinian, and other troops during the civil war, is thought to contain more than 100,000 unexploded landmines and other explosives. Visitors to the area are advised not to leave the main roads. Some regions are off-limits to visitors entirely. Go to www.vgsbooks.com for a link to the latest information about travel in Lebanon from the U.S. State Department.

AANJAR Aanjar, located in the Bekaa Valley, is a well-preserved Islamic town dating from the A.D. 700s. It is one of Lebanon's only remaining towns from this era. Visitors can see remains of the old city's walls, streets, columns, and brickwork, along with a public bathhouse, mosaics, and carvings. The partially reconstructed Great Palace is particularly intriguing.

BAALBEK This small town in the foothills of the Anti-Lebanon Mountains was a winter resort area in Roman times, when its name was Heliopolis—"City of the Sun." The town's vast ruins include an acropolis (hilltop temple), an early Christian church, and imposing temples to the Roman gods Bacchus and Jupiter. Visitors flock here every year for the famous Baalbek Festival, during which world-renowned musicians perform against a backdrop of dramatic temple ruins.

AL-BASS ARCHAEOLOGICAL SITE Located in Tyre, this site features extensive Roman ruins. Examples include a necropolis (tomb complex) and an aqueduct that once carried water to the city. Most impressive is the huge, well-preserved hippodrome, or stadium, which once seated approximately twenty thousand spectators. The Romans used to hold chariot races here.

BEITEDDINE PALACE Located in Beiteddine in the Chouf Mountains, this magnificent palace was built in the late 1700s and early 1800s as the headquarters for Bashir Shihab, Lebanon's Ottoman-appointed governor. The imposing palace is built high on a mountaintop overlooking the Bekaa Valley, surrounded by beautiful terraces, gardens, and orchards. Highlights include extensive mosaics, courtyards, and fountains. The palace was damaged during the civil war but has since been restored.

BYBLOS RUINS Byblos is one of the world's oldest inhabited towns, and visitors here can see ruins of ancient buildings dating to 5000 B.C. Each successive group of residents left its mark on the town: there are wall foundations dating to the Stone Age; Phoenician-era temples and fortifications; an Egyptian-era necropolis; a Roman theater; a Crusader castle; and a medieval town, among other structures.

CHOUF CEDAR RESERVE This 12,300-acre (5,000-hectare) reserve contains six cedar forests, including a number of ancient trees—some of which may be more than 1,500 years old. In addition to the magnificent cedars, the reserve serves as a home to wolves, gazelles, wild boars, and other animal life. There are also several old fortresses and shrines in the reserve. Hiking trails wind through the area.

JEITA GROTTO This natural cave complex near the Kalb River features an impressive display of stalactites and stalagmites. The caves stretch deep into the mountains for several miles, with vast chambers and fantastic rock formations. Some of the lower caves flood in winter. Depending on the time of year, visitors can view the caves on foot or by boat.

NATIONAL MUSEUM Dating to 1937, Lebanon's National Museum in Beirut was damaged during the civil war, but it reopened in 1999. Each era in Lebanese history is represented here, with examples from the Phoenician, Egyptian, Roman, Byzantine, Greek, and Mamluk periods. Visitors will see centuries- and millenniums-old mosaics, carvings, and statues, as well as jewelry, mirrors, coins, weapons, and other everyday objects from the ancient world.

TRIPOLI The northern city of Tripoli contains dozens of historic sights and attractions. Perhaps most intriguing are its many medieval mosques. Many of the mosques include distinctive minarets, or towers; enchanting courtyards and gardens; ornate facades (fronts); attractive black and white stonework; and dramatic domed and vaulted ceilings. Tripoli also has numerous madrassas, or Muslim religious schools; Crusader-era castles; and bustling souks.

archaeologist: a scientist who studies the remains of past human cultures

convert: to bring someone from one religious organization or belief into another

Druze: a member of a secretive religious group that broke off from Islam in the A.D. 1000s and remains active in Modern Lebanon

erosion: the wearing away of soil or rock by the action of wind, water, or ice

gross domestic product (GDP): the value of the goods and services produced by a country over a period of time, such as one year

guerrilla warfare: unconventional warfare carried out by small groups of combatants, often involving bombings and other terror tactics to frighten and kill civilians

hydroelectricity: electricity created by the power of rushing water. People often dam rivers to create hydroelectric power stations.

inflation: a steady rise in the prices of goods and services

Islam: a religion founded in the seventh century A.D. and based on the prophet Muhammad's teachings. Islam's holy book is the Quran.

literacy: the ability to read and write

Maronite: a member of a branch of Christianity that broke away from the mainstream Christian church in the A.D. 400s and remains active in modern Lebanon

militia: a small local army, usually not connected with an official government-run army

Quran: the holy book of Islam. The writings of the Quran were set forth by the Prophet Muhammad starting in 610. Muslims believe Allah (God) revealed these writings to Muhammad.

Shiite: a member of one of the two major Islamic sects. Shiites believe that only direct descendants of Muhammad's family are legitimate Islamic rulers.

Sunni: a member of one of the two major Islamic sects. Sunnis believe that Muhammad's successors can be chosen from among his closest colleagues and not necessarily from his direct relations.

Western: European or North American in outlook, culture, and tradition

Central Intelligence Agency (CIA). "Lebanon." *The World Factbook.*
2003.
<http://www.odci.gov/cia/publications/factbook/geos/le.html> (November 2003)
The World Factbook provides basic information on Lebanon's geography,
people, government, economy, communications, transportation, military, and
transnational issues.

Collelo, Thomas, ed. *Lebanon: A Country Study.* Washington, DC:
Federal Research Division, Library of Congress, 1989.
This comprehensive title examines Lebanon in depth, including its history,
geography, and society. While the political and economic sections are not up
to date, the rest of the book provides a wealth of detailed information.

Embassy of Lebanon. *Profile of Lebanon.* 2002.
<http://www.lebanonembassyus.org> (May 2004)
The Lebanese Embassy in Washington, D.C., provides a variety of information
about the nation, with pages devoted to history and culture, statistical data,
the economy, government, and the national anthem. There's a special "kids
only" section offering material of interest to young people.

Friedman, Thomas L. *From Beirut to Jerusalem.* New York:
Doubleday, 1989.
This best-selling title looks at the complexities of Middle Eastern politics,
with extensive information on the civil war in Lebanon and the Israeli-
Palestinian conflict.

Jenkins, Siona, and Ann Jousiffe. *Lebanon.* Melbourne, Australia:
Lonely Planet Publications, 2001.
This guidebook for travelers to Lebanon contains extensive information on the
nation's history, culture, geography, and attractions.

Mackey, Sandra. *Lebanon: Death of a Nation.* New York: Congdon
and Weed, Inc., 1989.
The author explores the complicated political and religious divisions that led
to civil war in Lebanon. She explains how the nation fell from prosperity into
chaos in the late twentieth century.

Oz, Amos. *The Slopes of Lebanon.* San Diego: Harcourt Brace
Jovanovich, Publishers, 1987.
This collection of essays by Israeli writer Amos Oz, a leader in the Israeli
peace movement, includes writings on Israel's raid into Lebanon in 1982.

*The Statesman's Yearbook: The Politics, Cultures, and Economies of
the World 2003.* New York: Palgrave Publishers Ltd., 2003.
This source presents a variety of statistics on Lebanese society, government,
industry, communications, and culture. It also includes a discussion of key
historical events.

U.S. Department of State. *Background Note: Lebanon.* 2002.
<http://www.state.gov/r/pa/ei/bgn/5419.htm>
This on-line resource offers extensive information about Lebanon's people,
government, history, political situation, and more.

Amari, Suad. *Cooking the Lebanese Way.* Minneapolis: Lerner Publications Company, 2003.
Revised and expanded, this easy-to-use cookbook features tasty Lebanese recipes, along with information on Lebanon's history, land, and customs.

Arabia GIS. *Lebanon Atlas.*
<http://www.lebanonatlas.com>
This fact-filled site offers abundant information about Lebanon, including profiles of major cities, tourist information, and maps.

Cedarland.
<http://www.cedarland.org>
This thorough website offers extensive information about Lebanon's history, along with a variety of cultural material.

Daily Star. *Daily Star On Line.*
<http://www.dailystar.com.lb>
The *Daily Star* is Lebanon's leading English-language newspaper. Readers can find up-to-date political news here, along with editorials, weather reports, and classified ads.

Gibran, Kahlil. *The Prophet.* 1923. Reprint, New York: Knopf, 1995.
Originally published in 1923, this inspirational book is the most famous work from Lebanon's most famous writer. The book offers insights into love, marriage, children, work, joy, sorrow, friendship, and more.

Hutchinson, Linda. *Lebanon.* San Diego: Lucent Books, 2003.
This title presents thorough information about Lebanon's history, culture, and political situation. The text is accompanied by black-and-white photos.

Katz, Samuel M. *Jerusalem or Death: Palestinian Terrorism.* Minneapolis: Lerner Publications Company, 2004.
This book offers a detailed look at Palestinian terrorist groups, which draw many members from the Palestinian refugee camps in Lebanon. The book covers the history, key issues, and people involved.

Markoe, Glenn E. *Phoenicians.* Berkeley: University of California Press, 2001.
This lavishly illustrated book examines the culture and history of Phoenicia, an ancient civilization based in modern-day Lebanon. The book includes, maps, drawings, and photographs of artifacts and excavations, accompanied by fact-filled text.

McDaniel, Jan. *Lebanon.* Broomall, PA: Mason Crest Publishers, 2003.
This well-illustrated title explores Lebanon's history, economy, government, and people. It also looks at Lebanon's major cities.

Further Reading and Websites

Nuweihed, Jamal Sleem. *Abu Jmeel's Daughter and Other Stories: Arab Folk Tales from Palestine and Lebanon.* **Northampton, MA: Interlink Publishing Group, 2001.**
This collection consists of twenty-seven enchanting Arab folk stories. Jamal Sleem Nuweihed, a novelist, had lovingly told these tales to her children and other family members for many years. She wrote them down shortly before her death.

vgsbooks.com.
<http://www.vgsbooks.com>
Visit vgsbooks.com, the homepage of the Visual Geography Series®. You can get linked to all sorts of useful on-line information, including geographical, historical, demographic, cultural, and economic websites. The vgsbooks.com site is a great resource for late-breaking news and statistics.

Captions for photos appearing on cover and chapter openers:

Cover: In the 60s B.C., Romans constructed a stadium in Tyre where horse and chariot races were held. Modern high-rise buildings can be seen through a crumbling archway of the Roman stadium.

pp. 4–5 Christian invaders built Sidon's Sea Castle (lower left) in the early 1200s on a small island. A stone bridge (lower right) connects it to the mainland.

pp. 8–9 Rugged cliffs and ravines characterize the Lebanon Mountains.

pp. 20–21 Phoenician cargo ships appear on this Assyrian stone carving created in the 700s B.C. for the palace of King Sargon II at Khorsabad (in modern Iraq). The ships are thought to be hauling cedar logs from Phoenicia (modern Lebanon) for use in constructing an Assyrian royal palace.

pp. 40–41 Some Druze women wear bright white veils. Other Lebanese women wear Western clothing exclusively.

pp. 46–47 An art gallery in Beirut displays a dark canvas lavishly embroidered with Arabic calligraphy (lettering).

pp. 58–59 Cranes remove containers of dry cement mix and other construction materials from a ship docked at Beirut.

Photo Acknowledgments
The images in this book are used with the permission of: © Art Directors/ Helene Rogers, pp. 4–5, 8–9, 10, 13, 43, 45, 46–47, 49, 51, 52, 55, 56, 58–59, 60, 61, 62, 63, 64; © Digital Cartographics, pp. 6, 11; Israeli Tsvika/The State of Israel National Photo Collection, p. 14; © Jane Sweeney/Art Directors, p. 17; © SuperStock, p. 18; Library of Congress, pp. 20–21 (LC-USZ6-929), 23 (LC-USZ62-93859), 28 (LC-USZC4-3493); © Paul Almasy/CORBIS, p. 24; © Carmen Redondo/CORBIS, p. 26; © Bettmann/CORBIS, p. 31; Burg El Barajneh/United Nations Relief and Works Agency, p. 32; © Art Directors/ Mark Gleeson, p. 33; Myrtle Winter Chaumeny/United Nations Relief and Works Agency, p. 34; Sa-ar Ya'acov/The State of Israel National Photo Collection; © Art Directors/TRIP, pp. 40–41; © Hanan Isachar/CORBIS, p. 48; courtesy of Mr. & Mrs. Kahlil Gibran, p. 50; www.banknotes.com, p. 68 (all).

Cover: © Art Directors/Helene Rogers. Back cover photo: NASA.